The Strength of a Free Mind

Meditations for the Accused

Kent H. Roberts

Published in the United States of America
ISBN-13: 978-1502853295
ISBN-10: 1502853299

Library of Congress Control Number: 2014918667
CreateSpace Independent Publishing Platform
North Charleston, South Carolina

Contents

Introduction

I was the top lawyer of a large technology company. My company accused me of criminal activity. In 2006 I was fired and publicly denounced for what was called an "improper incident." In 2007 I was indicted by the US Department of Justice and sued by the US Securities and Exchange Commission.

I needed help, more help than my lawyers could give me. The help I was seeking did not lie inside me, although I had much to do. I turned, as many do, to my faith. I am a Christian. As I reexamined Christian teaching and common experience in the light of my new needs, I found the direction and comfort I needed to meet the challenges I was facing. Although a Christian, I would take help where I could get it. When I became aware of anything relevant from American popular culture; world literature; or the Jewish, Hindu, or Muslim holy books, I was happy to consider it. The experience of being falsely accused is universal and persistent.

This book is designed for a person accused of wrongdoing, criminal or otherwise, and for anyone who has been mistreated, attacked, or excluded. I was innocent, and that sometimes figures prominently in the discussion, but I believe there is also much help here for a person who deserves the accusation, in whole or part. Being accused is a wrenching experience, and there is a lot to deal with.

This is a short book, but it is meant to be read slowly. The book is written in the form of a devotional. Chapters are called Meditations, a reference to the ancient prayer, "Let the words of my mouth and the meditation of my heart be acceptable to you, O Lord,* my rock and my redeemer." In each Meditation, a scripture is read, and then some relevant thoughts are offered. The reader adds the most important step by pondering his or her current concerns in the light of the readings and by taking those concerns to God in prayer. No matter what anybody else thinks of you, God loves you and wants to hear from you.

This book is not a memoir. I do not recount all my experiences, nor do I offer them in chronological order. My experience is important to another accused person only to the extent it opens up and begins contemplation upon the reader's own ongoing experience.

This book is not legal advice on how to respond to the various choices the accused will have to make. My case is my case. Yours is yours. I *will* endorse the view of a character in Charles Dickens's *Bleak House* concerning her falsely accused friend who intended to face a serious criminal charge without a lawyer: "'It won't do to have truth and justice on his side; he must have law and lawyers,' exclaim[ed] the old girl, apparently persuaded that the latter form a separate establishment, and have dissolved partnership with truth and justice for ever and a day."

This book is for those accused from one who has been there. In these Meditations there will be one message: In your troubles you are not alone. God is with you.

---

* In the scriptures quoted from here forward, God is frequently referred to as "the Lord." The name is printed in all capitals following a tradition in English going back at least to the King James Version (KJV) of the Bible in 1611. The KJV translators used "the Lord" as a substitute word for the divine name "YHWH." This follows an older Jewish tradition that the actual name of God is too holy to be spoken. By using the phrase "the Lord," the translators were attempting to convey the transcendence of God rather than limiting God to specific political, geographical or sexual characteristics. However, when human words are used to describe the divine, the process of shrinking the understanding of the divine seems inevitably to occur. I hope that these quotes and the discussion will be read in the light of the original intention and that any cultural connotations that have arisen since will be overlooked.

LORD, one who desires perfection must make it his first task to keep his mind at all times set on heavenly things. By so doing, he can pass carefree through many troubles, not as one who has not the wit to realize the dangers that beset him, but in the strength of a free mind, unfettered by undue attachments to worldly things.

Thomas á Kempis, The Imitation of Christ

one

Help!

I am the scorn of all my adversaries, a horror to my neighbors, an object of dread to my acquaintances; those who see me in the street flee from me. (Psalm 31:11)

When I was indicted on seven counts of fraud by the US government, I was facing potentially 140 years in prison. I needed help! Over a weekend I had been thrown into a bewildering new reality marked by confusion, embarrassment, isolation, anger, and fear. Every day, events and emotions invited me to turn to self-pity and despair. These were not legal issues; they were issues of the spirit.

Where could I turn for help?

I go to a wonderful church with a century-long history of ministry to the poor and unfortunate. The church has a large staff just for pastoral care to attend to the personal crises that inevitably occur within a ten-thousand-plus-member congregation. The ministers are extraordinary, and I wouldn't have a second thought about going to them with almost any problem.

I thought about talking to them, but the risks were real and overwhelming. With good reason I feared FBI agents following behind me, subjecting my pastors to interrogation, using all their coercive power and creativity to try to break the confessional privilege in hopes of finding something to prove the government's case against me.

This prospect was even worse for my friends and family, where the law provides no protection from examination by the government. During this time in a case similar to mine, federal agents threatened to interrogate a thirteen-year-old boy to try to get evidence against his father, who was being accused of securities fraud.

I also knew that being under indictment is not a situation that is easy to relate to. I was distressed and did not want my friends, family, and pastors to say something unintentionally hurtful to me, damaging those important relationships. I looked for pastoral writings on counseling the accused and found none.

Finally, I didn't know what the persons I sought out for counseling would think. Would they join the chorus of accusation against me? On the Sunday after I was indicted, my wife and I stopped cold in the church parking lot, briefly unable to decide whether we should go in. In some cultures there is an automatic compassion for the accused. The person's situation is called his or her "troubles." In our culture indictment is tantamount to conviction, and there is strong faith in the justice system. "Where there's smoke, there must be fire." My brother-in-law told me about his father, who was imprisoned for months pending trial for a crime he did not commit. The government had a videotape of him not committing the crime! Ultimately, the charges were dropped, but if he had been convicted – innocent or not – his particular religion would have excommunicated him.

Where could I turn for help?

I found my help from the accused. I didn't have to say much for them to know what was happening around me and inside me. I sought out a friend who had an IRS problem years before. Another friend who unknown to me had faced but avoided federal indictment sought me out. I began reading the experiences of others (especially in Russia). I discovered that the Bible is *rich* with directly relevant information for the accused. Jesus and Paul and, before them, Joseph, Moses, David, Elijah, Jeremiah, and John the Baptist had been accused.

Most important, God sought me out and did what God could – which was quite a lot.

The first thing you need to know is the thing I learned: In your troubles you are not alone. God is with you.

two

Bewildered

More in number than the hairs of my head are those who hate me without cause; many are those who would destroy me, my enemies who accuse
me falsely. What I did not steal must I now restore? (Psalm 69:4)

After I was fired, I had a lot of time to drive my teenage daughter to
her various activities. I overheard many of her phone calls. When the
conversation took an unexpected turn, she interjected, "Wait! What?" I
thought it was a sweet and elegant expression of bewilderment.

As a newly accused person, I was feeling a lot of bewilderment. At
the time I compared it to being "sucked into a vortex." I was profoundly
disoriented. My first thoughts were that there was some government-
induced panic happening and they momentarily forgot who I was. A
criminal? *Hey, it's* me *you are talking about. You know I am the opposite
of a criminal.* Then I racked my memory. I recalled all I could about
the incidents in question. My memories didn't convict me. *But wait*, I
said, turning briefly on myself, *what if my memories are wrong?* That
was its own black hole. But how could I commit a crime and not be profoundly aware of it, at least at the emotional level? I have a pretty noisy
conscience, and it was hard for me to imagine, even in my distress and
disorientation, that I inadvertently committed a crime.

Then I started looking at the criminal code, and the free fall started
again. I was reasonably well trained in criminal law as it stood in about

1980. I found out that there was now a crime called theft of "honest services." I read the statute to get more information. The statute had no information at all about what set of actions Congress made into a crime. All it said was that if you do it – whatever it is – you spend twenty years in prison and pay a five-million-dollar fine. The statute was infinitely malleable in the prosecutor's hands. Presumably, a person "stole" the "expectation of honest services" from his or her employer. During this time, a fellow in my church was sent to prison for "stealing" the "expectation of honest services" from a company he didn't even work for. He spent nine months there before the appeals court freed him, saying his conviction was a misuse of a statute that is so "vague and amorphous on its face" that its meaning can only be "divined from a jumble of disparate cases."

That explained how my instincts and training might have failed me – there were now statutes so vague that they permitted ambitious prosecutors to make a person a criminal for doing – or not doing – what that person could not have known was criminal at the time. The vortex took a sharp and frightening turn toward cynicism. I had heard about this type of legal system in middle school. At the height of the Cold War, I studied totalitarianism. The Soviet novelist Vasily Grossman commented on the German state: "National Socialism had created a new type of political criminal: criminals who had not committed a crime." I quickly put this aside, as there was no immediate value to me in this line of thought.

Faced with turbulent uncertainty and under heavy pressure, I had to start making decisions – decisions with huge consequences.

The great Christian writer Thomas á Kempis wrote, "Times of trouble best discover the true worth of a man; they do not weaken him, but show his true nature."

Fundamentally, the accused is faced with a basic choice. Will you seek the approval of God or the approval of society? As strange as it may seem, society deeply wants you – the accused – to agree with its judgment. The government has guns, prisons, and nuclear bombs, but what it really wants is your consent. To obtain it, the government will offer you inducements. It will hail you – and deduct "points" from your penalty under the sentencing guidelines – if you "take responsibility." If you don't consent, they will amp up the threats. When I turned down a no prison time plea bargain deal, the prosecutor sent me a letter detailing the government's intention to put me in prison for many years. The government also offers an array of bonus programs if you go to work for it as a cooperating witness.

There are cases where the approval of God and society might dictate the same set of actions. For me, an innocent person, this was not one of those cases. At the end of the day, I decided I would bear false witness if I admitted to a crime I didn't commit, and in violation of the Golden Rule, I would make it easier for the government to roll over the next innocent person.

One of the spectacles of acquiescence that the system stages is the convicted defendant's plea for mercy at the sentencing hearing. It is set up so that even an innocent person has an incentive to "take responsibility" for *something* to curry favor with the judge. I have studied some of these speeches. The best was made by the apostle Paul in the Bible.

Paul was wrongly accused, which started a long legal process that resulted in his torture and execution in Rome under the emperor Nero. Paul said, "But with me it is a very small thing that I should be judged by you or by any human court. I do not even judge myself. I am not aware of anything against myself, but I am not thereby acquitted. It is the LORD who judges me. Therefore do not pronounce judgment before the time, before the LORD comes, who will bring to light the things now hidden in darkness and will disclose the purposes of the heart. Then each one will receive commendation from God."

In making whatever decisions you make, worry about the commendation of God.

three

Underwater

One day he got into a boat with his disciples, and he said to them, "Let us
go across to the other side of the lake." So they put out, and while they
were sailing he fell asleep. A windstorm swept down on the lake, and the
boat was filling with water, and they were in danger. They went to him
and woke him up, shouting, "Master, master, we are perishing!" And he
woke up and rebuked the wind and the raging waves; they ceased, and there
was a calm. He said to them, "Where is your faith?" (Luke 8:22–25)

Being indicted and tried is a memorable experience – not memorable
in the positive sense of "those were days to remember," but memorable
in the literal sense of you will never be able to forget it. Looking back, I
am a little surprised that I never asked myself how I wanted to remember this experience. I think this is because I was in the same state of
mind as the disciples in the story from the Gospel of Luke. Like a person
about to be thrown in deep water, I was distressed and could only think
about finding safety. Finding safety when underwater requires figuring
out which way is up and then where the shore is. In other words, it is
first about getting oriented. I think the question of how one wants to
remember this experience is useful for gaining perspective so that the
accused can make the choices that must be made.

After I was indicted, my family and I watched a movie called
Freedom Writers about a teacher's experiences in a gang-riddled high
school in Long Beach, California. In the opening sequence, the police

subdue and handcuff a Hispanic man in the living room of his house as his nine-year-old daughter watches. He is innocent of the crime, but he will be convicted and sentenced to life in prison for it. On the floor he looks up at his daughter. His look is devastating. His eyes don't express pain or shame. If anything he gives a look of instruction to his daughter, seeming to say, "Do you see and understand? This is how it is."

I really had to struggle to accept the insight "this is how it is." It felt too small for my circumstances. At times I felt like I was the first person - certainly in my neighborhood - to experience unjust arrest, indictment, and trial.

I know I am not the only one who has felt this way. In the movie the fellow from Long Beach was right. The wave that caught me is part of a flood that has been devastating other parts of society for a long time.

Many times I wanted to make a grand, fiery speech that would be published in the national newspapers pointing out the injustices of my case and demonstrating the scary vulnerability all citizens face before the wayward machinery of American justice. The people would rise up! My accusers would slink away in shame! I would be a hero! I carried a handwritten draft of this speech around for months. Fortunately, cooler heads prevailed. It is painful to remember.

My tendency to grandiosity was an effort to develop a point of reference to understand what was happening. Others might be motivated by the need for security, for certainty, or to control others. Perspective is necessary. That is what getting oriented is all about. So, again, how do you want to remember this experience? This question is intimately linked with the question, how are you going to act?

Grandiosity can lead to horrible choices. Alcoholics Anonymous founder Bill Wilson struggled with grandiosity and his own sense of importance. This led him first to alcohol and later to debilitating depression. To reduce the risk of grandiosity, he made anonymity "the spiritual foundation" of the Twelve Traditions of Alcoholics Anonymous.

Wilson tied the issue of grandiosity directly to the issue of approval seeking. He wrote, "My basic flaw has always been dependence – almost absolute dependence – on people or circumstances to supply me with prestige, security and the like. Failing to get these things according to my perfectionistic dreams and specifications, I had fought for them. And when defeat came, so did my depression."

Thus, there is a deeper, underlying question: whose approval will you seek?

The Gospel of John tells a sad story about approval seeking and the pursuit of glory. The teaching of Jesus initially had wide appeal across all social classes. Many prominent, respected persons became followers. John reports, "Nevertheless many, even of the authorities, believed in him. But because of the Pharisees [a powerful Jewish group] they did not confess it, for fear that they would be put out of the synagogue; for they loved human glory more than the glory that comes from God." Given a choice, these new followers of Jesus chose to seek the approval of their neighbors rather than to trust God.

In the story about the windstorm on the lake from the Gospel of Luke, Jesus awoke in response to the disciples' panicked pleas, calmed the water, and then turned to the disciples and asked, "Where is your faith?" Considering that they were still floating in a boat in highly changeable weather, Jesus's question is not a rebuke. Rather, he is inviting the disciples to decide what they will trust in a crisis.

Where is your faith? In your choices seek the approval of God. In the end that is the only glory that counts.

four

Embarrassed

Blessed are the poor in spirit, for theirs is the kingdom of heaven.
Blessed are those who mourn, for they will be comforted.
Blessed are the meek, for they will inherit the earth. (Matthew 5:3-5)

I was indicted on seven counts of fraud and other crimes by the United States on a Tuesday. The next day, the US Securities and Exchange Commission sued me for securities violations. From that Wednesday through Saturday, many lengthy articles discussing my alleged crimes appeared in *The Wall Street Journal; The New York Times; USA Today;* the local newspapers in Silicon Valley and Dallas, where I live; and the nationwide legal newspapers, like *The American Lawyer.* The articles provided Internet links to the indictment and the SEC complaint for those who wanted to know more.

The next Monday, I was to appear in San Francisco (where my trial would take place) for the initial hearing before the trial judge. At the airport I needed to make an adjustment in my flight plans. I left my ticket with the gate attendant. She was to call my name on the loud speaker when she had the information she needed to make the change. I had done this dozens of times before.

Suddenly, I thought about her broadcasting my name. I looked around the packed waiting area. I did not want the gate attendant to call out my name because I did not want someone to look up at me and say,

"Is it *that* Kent Roberts?" I did not want to be associated with my own blackened name. I made that panicky-looking move where you start off in one direction, halt abruptly, and quickly return to your original position. I was embarrassed. The Psalmist prayed for me when he said, "You [LORD] know the insults I receive, and my shame and dishonor."

Shortly afterward, I read the following in *The Imitation of Christ*: "It is good, too, that we sometimes suffer opposition, and that men think ill of us and misjudge us, even when we do and mean well. Such things are an aid to humility, and preserve us from pride and vainglory. For we more readily turn to God as our inward witness, when men despise us and think no good of us. A man should therefore place such complete trust in God, that he has no need of comfort from men."

I was ready to hear this.

Being under indictment is without question a dark and gathering cloud. Take a moment, though, to appreciate this one silver lining. God knows, even better than you, where you really stand with regard to the charges against you. God, not any jury or court (or reporter, blogger, or editorial writer), will be your ultimate judge. God will be with you when you are scorned and abandoned by others – especially then.

In the first three Beatitudes, Jesus outlines the rich blessings available to those who turn from the pride and priorities of the world. The world has turned from you. Rather than chasing after its approval, consider the advantages of trusting in God.

Now is a good time to turn to God as your inward witness and source of comfort.

five

Abandoned

At my first defense no one came to my support, but all deserted me. May it not be counted against them! (2 Timothy 4:16)

One of the many hurtful things about being accused is that many friends, coworkers, and family pull back. This reaction is not unique or even new. Three thousand years ago, King David lamented, "I am the scorn of all my adversaries, a horror to my neighbors, an object of dread to my acquaintances; those who see me in the street flee from me." I felt this abandonment intensely. Of all people, those who knew me should have believed that there was another side to the story. I muttered about "fair-weather friends" and resolved that when this was over, these relationships would have to be seriously reconsidered.

There are still some people on my "fair-weather friend" list. I still struggle to put fully into practice the insight that there is a world of difference between betrayal and mere abandonment in a dangerous time.

Jesus and the apostle Paul experienced abandonment by friends and followers. Paul noted that "all deserted me" and then exclaimed, "May it not be counted against them!"

Just before he was arrested, Jesus told his followers, "You will all become deserters because of me." The story of Peter's three denials of Jesus that night is frequently discussed. Looking at the matter from the perspective of the accused, Peter's actions are more complex than usually presented from the pulpit or in Sunday school.

Jesus knew that he was about to be thrown under the heel of the Roman Empire. When telling his disciples how they would react, Jesus made reference to the Old Testament proverb "Strike the shepherd, that the sheep may be scattered." Jesus was on sound psychological ground.

Not just Peter but all the disciples vowed they would never deny or desert Jesus.

When the soldiers came for Jesus, Peter stepped forward to defend Jesus. He drew his sword and injured the high priest's slave. Jesus told Peter to put away his sword.

As the trial of Jesus progressed through the night, only Peter and one other disciple braved the gathering crowd to follow the proceedings. At one point Peter even "sat with the guards in order to see how this would end."

Later that night Peter indeed denied he knew Jesus three times before he caught a glimpse of Jesus early the next morning.

Of that encounter the scripture says, "The LORD turned and looked at Peter." Peter's response is captured. He was shattered and "went out and wept bitterly." Jesus's response is not recorded. The preachers usually guess that Jesus was disappointed or, at best, tolerated Peter's weakness. As one who has been accused, I think that Jesus's response was likely different. After a long night of ridicule and false accusation, Jesus sees, among the murderous crowd, the face of his dear friend Peter. There is every reason to believe that Peter, imperfect as he was, comforted Jesus at a critical time by his presence alone.

Peter's next actions show his love for Jesus was undiminished after Jesus was crucified. Two days later when startling news came that Jesus had risen from the dead, "Peter got up and ran to the tomb." He climbed all the way into the tomb and saw that the burial dressings of Jesus had been carefully rolled up and placed to the side. A little later, Peter and the other disciples returned to Galilee. They were fishing when Jesus appeared to them, as he had promised. Peter didn't wait for the boat to get ashore. He "put on some clothes...and jumped into the sea."

Sitting on the beach after breakfast, Jesus and Peter communed without acrimony. In fact, Jesus reached out to Peter as a fellow sufferer. He said, "[W]hen you grow old, you will stretch out your hands, and someone else will fasten a belt around you and take you where you do not wish to go." John noted that "(He said this to indicate the kind of death by which he would glorify God.)" It was a moment of grim and pure brotherhood. Decades later, Peter was bound and publicly executed in Rome for being a follower of Jesus.

The truth is, you don't know how you would act if the situation were reversed and it was your so-called "fair-weather friend" who was accused. This is a time for patience and understanding.

It is a time to celebrate those who step forward at all – however uncertainly.

six

Betrayed

Now the chief priests and the whole council were looking for testimony against
Jesus to put him to death; but they found none. For many gave false testimony against him, and their testimony did not agree. (Mark 14:55–56)

After my troubles with the government were over, I attended a day in
the trial of a business executive accused of twenty counts of fraud. For
the jury to find fraud, the government had to show that there was hiding of information and that the executive was sneaking about. The main
witness against the executive was a fellow executive he had worked
closely with for two decades.

Listening to the witness's testimony that day, one could form a dis-
turbing understanding about what was happening. He testified that he
and the accused had acted secretly, without authorization, and without
the knowledge of the company's accountants and that they both knew
they were doing wrong.

The witness confirmed that he met with the FBI about two dozen
times before trial. The first five times, he told the FBI that the decisions in question were authorized and openly communicated to all con-
cerned and that both he and the accused felt they were acting within
permissible bounds. The statements made by the witness in the initial
five interviews closely matched the contemporaneous documents. In
other words, these earlier statements looked like the truth.

The testimony suggested that after the initial interviews, the witness was threatened with a substantial prison term that would have left his young children without a healthy caregiver. He then entered into a plea agreement to cooperate with the government in exchange for a lighter sentence. His testimony changed to what was heard at trial.

To betray someone is to misappropriate his or her life for your own purposes. According to the King James Version, Jesus makes reference to "them which despitefully use you." Whether out of spite or fear, to shield themselves or settle some old score, betrayers seek to diminish your future in order to improve or preserve their own. The novel *The Poisonwood Bible* captures the betrayer's mind-set. In it a preacher has a remarkable wife and four daughters, three of which are also remarkable. The fourth daughter, though completely average, is the most materially successful. Late in life, she muses on her operating principle: "Sometimes I really do think I owe the secret of my success to that little book I read long ago called *How to Survive 101 Calamities*. Simple remedies for dire situations, that's the lesson. In a falling elevator, try to climb up on the person nearby so their body will cushion your landing."

The prevalence of dishonesty in the criminal justice system is a shock to those who come into close contact with it for the first time. The prosecutors in the case I watched frequently bristled at any suggestion that they had behaved improperly. They may have been honestly unable to see the difference between what they wanted to hear and the truth.

It is true that the criminal justice system does not just tolerate betrayal. It promotes and rewards betrayal. It is true that the system in this country is not unique in that respect and that there are other systems that are much worse. This does not excuse the betrayer, and it does not excuse the person who rewards the betrayer.

The Bible's view on this point is clear. "You shall not bear false witness against your neighbor." God did not stop with the creator of the false report. "You shall not spread a false report." Today, the legal ethics rules of every state prohibit a lawyer from knowingly offering false evidence in court.

When the Book of Deuteronomy was reread in the late seventh century BC, the king of Judah instituted special procedures to eliminate false testimony. God said this was to be done "So you shall purge the evil from your midst. The rest shall hear and be afraid, and a crime such as this shall never again be committed among you." Alas, these reforms were soon abandoned.

Jesus held the same stark views about betrayal. At the Last Supper, he spoke of his coming betrayal with Judas Iscariot present. Jesus said, "[W]oe to that one by whom the Son of Man is betrayed! It would have been better for that one not to have been born."

Betrayal is a potent word, and it should not be overused, but I was betrayed, and it is very possible that you will be betrayed.

The message I would give you here is not one of forgiveness, but one of restraint. Cooperating witnesses are sometimes created under pressure. Sometimes, like Judas Iscariot, they just voluntarily walk into the authorities from off the street. Sometimes anger is used to motivate a cooperator. Watch out for efforts to use your anger against you in order to make you a cooperating witness. Being a cooperating witness for the government is a lifetime position.

seven

Isolated

You are the light of the world. A city built on a hill cannot be hid. No one after lighting a lamp puts it under a bushel basket, but on the lampstand, and it gives light to all in the house. In the same way, let your light shine before others, so that they may see your good works and give glory to your Father in heaven. (Matthew 5:14–16)

The day after I was indicted, I went to court in San Francisco to enter a plea of not guilty. Taking my plea was one of many criminal matters being handled by the federal magistrate judge that morning. As a result both tables in the courtroom were filled with prosecutors.

As the morning progressed, I noticed that the junior prosecutor handling my case would not look at my face. I decided to find out if this was intentional. When it was time to go up to the judge to plead not guilty, I walked between the two tables full of prosecutors. I expectantly searched their faces for any recognition. Not a single one of them would look at me.

I quickly dismissed my first thought – that they were collectively ashamed to be doing this to an innocent man – and wondered whether there was a conscious policy to humiliate the criminal defendant by refusing to look him in the eye. Laurence Gonzales reports, "Psychologists have observed that one of the most basic human needs, beginning at birth, is to be gazed upon by another....To be seen is to be real, and without another to gaze upon us, we are nothing. Part of the terror of being lost stems from the idea of never being seen again."

I don't know whether there is an explicit policy to pretend not to see a defendant, but it is clearly a long-standing folk tradition. A third-century Christian bishop persecuted by the Romans said, concerning the way the Romans conducted the persecutions, "They were not to show the least consideration for us but to regard us and treat us as if we no longer existed, this being the second torture devised by our adversaries in addition to the floggings." Starting with the Great Terror of 1937, the Soviet dictator Stalin issued an order concerning his enemies: "We must finish with them, not looking at their faces." Solzhenitsyn, who was on the receiving end of Stalin's policy, confirmed, "No one... addressed a human word to you. No one had looked at you with a human gaze." This dehumanizing practice, which the Christian bishop called "the second torture," continues in modern American courtrooms.

In the Sermon on the Mount, Jesus said, "You have heard that it was said, 'An eye for an eye and a tooth for a tooth.' But I say to you...if anyone forces you to go one mile, go also a second mile." I was taught that Jesus was saying don't respond to provocation tit for tat, but make your response more constructive so as to "let your light shine before others... so that they may...give glory to your Father in heaven."

I had a number of possible responses. I could take it personally, as intended. I could become angry. Or I could elevate my response.

It seemed to me that the agents of my government were being rude, and I liked the idea that a little Southern courtesy was also an act of defiance.

The next week, at the first hearing on the Securities and Exchange Commission case against me, I walked over, extended my hand, and introduced myself to the two attorneys representing the SEC. They were a little startled. At my first meeting with the senior prosecutor in the criminal case, I did the same with her. She was able to lift her gaze all the way up to my mouth. In the following months, the etiquette was that we could not do more than greet each other. After a year though, the senior prosecutor would smile and wave when she saw me in the cafeteria before pretrial hearings.

By the time of trial, I was in such a state of mind that all I could pray for was that during the day I would act like a Christian. Even with the best lawyers in the world, I knew that everything was in God's hands. My wife was with me for the whole trial. Our daughter had come to San Francisco for jury selection and opening arguments. Then she had to go home to Dallas for school.

My wife and I were heading out of court after the third or fourth day of testimony and we found ourselves in the elevator with both of the prosecutors. It was naturally very awkward. I introduced them to my wife.

The junior prosecutor looked her in the eye; shook her hand; and said, "Hello, Mrs. Roberts."

The senior prosecutor took my wife's hand and said, "Hello, Mrs. Roberts. You have a beautiful daughter." I had to smile.

I did not let the government define me or dictate my response. You do not have to either. How you respond can send a powerful message. The father of my brother-in-law was indicted and could not make bail. He was imprisoned for months before the baseless charges against him were dropped. While in prison he prayed, read the scriptures, and acted the best he knew how. In honor of his humble spirit, his fellow inmates gave him the nickname "Moses."

Even though you are accused and vilified, "You are the light of the world...No one after lighting a lamp puts it under a bushel basket, but on the lampstand, and it gives light to all in the house."

eight

Lonely

Turn to me and be gracious to me, for I am lonely and afflicted. (Psalm 25:16)

This was a lonely experience. I felt cut off. I felt removed from society. I was surprised to find how directly the Bible addresses the loneliness of the accused.

The prophet Jeremiah lived and spoke in the Kingdom of Judah around the turn of the sixth century BC. His prophecies made powerful enemies. When he was accused of treason, "they took Jeremiah and threw him into the cistern...letting Jeremiah down by ropes. Now there was no water in the cistern, but only mud, and Jeremiah sank into the mud." An intensely social man, Jeremiah wrote frequently of his loneliness. This was his loneliest moment. Another time, he lamented, "I have become a laughingstock all day long; everyone mocks me...All my close friends are watching for me to stumble."

Even Jesus, at the most brutal moment in his execution, acknowledged the loneliness, calling out from the cross, "My God, my God, why have you forsaken me?"

For one accused of a crime, several things deepen the loneliness and isolation.

The government actually tries to isolate the accused. This serves both as a warning to others and to make the accused more vulnerable and open to the prosecutors' proposals for what they like to call "the prompt and efficient resolution of the case."

Employment issues can add to loneliness. Most Americans get too much of their self-worth from their jobs. If a person is unemployed or has had to change jobs in response to the accusation, he or she feels less worthy. Men in particular take too many of their friends from the ranks of their coworkers. When a person is fired, these relationships are altered or simply end. My former employer told my coworkers that they would be fired if they even talked to me.

After indictment I was provided with Federal Bureau of Investigation documents called "302s." These are memoranda of conversations with potential witnesses. Reading these, I began to see how things I said to my friends or former colleagues looked when imperfectly remembered or, worse, cynically twisted. Seeing this shut down conversation and relationships.

Being accused is a unique experience, and friends who haven't shared it can sometimes seem like the well-intentioned friends of Job of the Old Testament. Job was a "blameless and upright" man who experienced catastrophic reverses. His friends had plenty to say to him, but what they said wasn't just wrong, it was hurtful and beside the point. Like Job, the accused wants to pull away from such friends to preserve the relationship from their ignorance and his or her irritation. This compounds the loneliness.

Adding to Job's troubles, his wife abandoned him early. She ridiculed his claim of innocence, saying, "Do you still persist in your integrity? Curse God and die." Being accused puts an enormous strain on your marriage. The traditional wedding vows address the possibility of facing adversity together – "for richer and poorer, in sickness and in health" – but this situation is different. A friend of mine, who always knew the right thing to say, told me that in this regard I had it a lot better than Job. My wife was fully supportive, and I never doubted her love. Still, I felt some distance seeing how much distress the situation was causing my family. That added to my sense of loneliness.

The experience of Elijah, the greatest prophet in the Old Testament, suggests an important truth about loneliness. Elijah was sent by God to confront the idolatrous practices of King Ahab and Queen Jezebel who reigned in the northern Kingdom of Israel in the ninth century BC.

Following a demonstration of the power of the true God over her 450 false prophets, Jezebel imposed a death sentence on Elijah and he fled.

The fugitive prophet Elijah lamented to the LORD, "I alone am left, and they are seeking my life, to take it away." The scripture gives no reason to doubt Elijah's sincerity. In fact, Elijah repeats this statement – "I alone am left" – twice.

In his isolation Elijah failed to remember a few important facts. Before the conflict with the 450 prophets of Baal that resulted in his death sentence, Elijah had met with the chamberlain of the royal palace who "revered the LORD greatly." The chamberlain told Elijah in confidence that he had "hid[den] a hundred of the LORD's prophets fifty to a cave, and provided them with bread and water." At the great conflict itself, the Bible says "all the people [of Israel] fell on their faces and said, 'The LORD indeed is God; the LORD indeed is God.'"

The LORD brought Elijah to Mount Horeb and spoke to Elijah with "a still small voice." What God told him was that there were seven thousand still faithful in Israel. Elijah was not alone. He was lonely, but he was not alone.

Like Elijah, I was lonely. I am a little introverted, but this was a different type of isolation. I wanted to know what others in this situation felt and how they handled things, but I was fearful of reaching out.

Like Elijah, I was never really alone. God sought me out through the scriptures and through other people. The scriptures are filled with stories of persons who had dealt with the issues I was facing. Jesus faced them, too, and responded perfectly. Jesus faced them because he loves us! People I knew and people I didn't know sought me out to speak words of encouragement and support. I felt that they were prophets sent to me by God.

The same is true for you. You are not alone. You are just lonely. God is with you. Listen for the still small voice of God in this situation.

nine

Angry

Be angry but do not sin; do not let the sun go down on your anger,
and do not make room for the devil. (Ephesians 4:26–27)

The criminal justice system creates and sustains anger. A person who is falsely accused has every reason to be angry.

Anger is a God-given emotion. Each person has a fight-or-flight response to danger. Science writer Daniel Goleman points out that anger readies the body chemically to take the physical actions necessary in a fight for survival. As the cyborg the Terminator said, "Anger is more useful than despair."

Anger is also dangerous. The writer of Ecclesiastes warned, "Do not be quick to anger, for anger lodges in the bosom of fools." Jesus taught, "You have heard that it was said to those of old, 'You shall not murder,' and whoever murders will be in danger of the judgment. But I say to you that whoever is angry with his brother without a cause will be in danger of the judgment."

Anger can indeed lodge in the soul and take over. Mr. Goleman reports, "[A]nger is the mood people are worst at controlling. Indeed, anger is the most seductive of the negative emotions; the self-righteous inner monologue that propels it along fills the mind with the most convincing arguments for venting rage. Unlike sadness, anger is energizing, even exhilarating."

This is a very ancient problem, and the ancient writers have a lot of very intelligent things to say to an angry person.

The fact that a person becomes angry is never condemned. There are newer versions of the Bible that relegate the phrase "without a cause" in Jesus's teaching to a footnote, but the context is clear that he is talking about what you do with anger, not that you became angry. The apostle Paul, whose teachings never conflicted with those of Jesus, said, "Be angry but do not sin." The Psalmist describes the LORD as "slow to anger."

Anger must be managed. I keep a reminder of this truth in our living room. When I was in India teaching employees about the company's whistleblower hotline, I bought a beautiful sandalwood carving of the popular Hindu deity Ganesha. In Hindu sacred writing, Ganesha was a paunchy man who was decapitated by another deity. The other god then placed an elephant's head on Ganesha's body. What I like about the statue is that Ganesha is stepping on a rat. The salesman explained to me that the rat represents deep passion and the moral teaching of the story of Ganesha is that when the rat runs free – when passion is not kept under foot – it destroys everything, but when the rat is controlled – when passion is kept under foot – it propels us forward. Anger is a "rat" to be kept firmly under control.

It doesn't help things to vent anger uncontrollably. Giving voice to anger can kindle anger into rage. A prayer I still use daily is Psalm 4:4. In one version of the Bible, it reads, "Be angry, and do not sin. Meditate within your heart on your bed, and be still." In another version, it reads, "When you are disturbed, do not sin; ponder it on your beds, and be silent." This is not so easy in practice. During my time of troubles, I lost it once. That was in response to the nose-flaring, red-faced anger of another lawyer in the case. I took my attorney out of the conference room we were in and shared my feelings of outrage with him. Talking about it actually made me feel more inflamed, but at least I was silent to the other person. Not broadcasting your anger gives you time to work on it – to "ponder" or "meditate."

The scriptures teach that we must domesticate our anger. It arose to alert us to the need to deal with a situation. Move on to dealing with the situation. Anger fanned into rage can distract and lead a person to act against his or her own interests. That is what our mothers meant when they said, "Don't cut off your nose to spite your face." Solomon advised, "One who is slow to anger is better than the mighty, and one whose temper is controlled [is better] than one who captures a city."

Another Hebrew proverb says, "Whoever is slow to anger has great understanding, but one who has a hasty temper exalts folly."

Biologically, anger is a call to action. The goal is not to let anger "lodge in your bosom," but to move on to useful action. Paul told the Ephesians, "[D]o not let the sun go down on your anger, and do not make room for the devil."

My program for anger management was pretty simple. The foundation was prayer, especially prayer for my enemies. President Eisenhower said, "Don't go to war in response to emotions of anger and resentment; do it prayerfully." I meditated. This is different from mulling things over, which can open you up to the "self-righteous inner monologue" Goleman talked about. This is a mental discipline that permitted me to go from saying "I am angry" to saying "There is anger in me." I exercised. Aerobic exercise floods the body with oxygen. That increases the sense of well-being. When I exercise, I have to make a conscious choice to continue to dwell on my anger. I did my best to choose not to. Finally, I laughed. Anger and laughter come from two different places.

"Anger is more useful than despair." You have a hard battle to fight, so fight it, but move past the anger to focus on the battle itself. God will be with you in both tasks.

ten

Regret

Now all the tax collectors and sinners were coming near to listen to him. And the Pharisees and the scribes were grumbling and saying, "This fellow welcomes sinners and eats with them." (Luke 15:1–2)

In the days and weeks after I was abruptly fired, my former employer undertook a massive investigation. Teams of attorneys and forensic accountants sifted through all of my e-mails, files, and old expense reports looking for anything that could possibly be questioned. Months later, when I read through their work product, I was reassured about how I had conducted myself at work. I had always tried hard to act properly there. Certainly, despite their best efforts, they found nothing actually criminal and no violations of company policy.

Nevertheless, their report was a masterpiece of selective presentation and innuendo, and I was indicted on baseless charges.

While the company's investigation was going on, I undertook my own very wide-ranging inventory of my life. I went back three decades or more. The Soviet novelist Vasily Grossman observed, "Good men and bad men alike are capable of weakness. The difference is simply that a bad man will be proud all his life of one good deed – while an honest man is hardly aware of his good acts, but remembers a single sin for years on end."

I guess I would be classified as "an honest man" by Grossman's definition. I was not at all pleased with what I saw in my life. I am not talking about crimes. Before the crisis I was constantly away from my family on company travel I thought was necessary. One year, the company sent the employees' spouses a summary of employee benefits. My wife called me and wanted to know why, when I was entitled to more than a month's vacation annually based on my years of service, she had to beg me to take even a week-long vacation, and even then, I wouldn't turn off my cell phone. Also, although I had always been active in the church, at that time I was near dead spiritually. Like many, I reacted badly to what was happening in American Christianity. I forgot that Jesus was a lacerating critic of the church of his day but remained fully committed to God.

"Objectively, I am fine," I wrote in my personal journal a year before I was fired, but I also wrote the following: "I am at quite a low ebb spiritually. I do not like the church. I do not like Christianity. I am at the same time sinking morally. I used to be able to put anything in perspective. Now I am pessimistic and upset by change. I really don't like this."

The extent of my alienation felt like sin to me. Intuitively, we feel like some sins are not as bad as others. Still, sin is sin, and it separates us from God. The apostle Paul famously wrote, "For there is no distinction...all have sinned and fall short of the glory of God."

My spiritual state distressed me. Then a criticism made against Jesus caught my attention. It was a time when persons of low social status were flocking to hear him. "And the Pharisees and the scribes were grumbling and saying, 'This fellow welcomes sinners and eats with them.'"

Jesus "welcomes sinners and eats with them." I wanted to be welcomed. I wanted to be invited to dinner.

Wait! Why would Jesus invite sinners to dinner?

In another account of this story, Jesus answered the Pharisees, "Those who are well have no need of a physician, but those who are sick; I have come to call not the righteous but sinners."

Paul asked, "Do you not realize that God's kindness is meant to lead you to repentance?"

Repentance is turning away from sin and toward God.

The apostle Peter said, "Repent therefore, and turn to God so that your sins may be wiped out."

Repentance removes the illness Jesus talked about and we are transformed to health.

The Book of Ezekiel, written in Babylon during the sixth century BC, contains this promise made in the name of God: "Cast away from you all the transgressions that you have committed against me, and get yourselves a new heart and a new spirit!"

I seized on this promise with enthusiasm and without reservation. I turned sharply toward God. So should you. Repent and be healed.

However, since you are in the middle of resolving an accusation, there are a few more things that should be considered about moral inventories and repentance.

Sometimes, the moral inventory may cause you to realize that the accusation being made against you is true. The American evangelist Charles Colson initially gained fame as a lawyer in the White House during the Watergate scandal. While he was a target of federal prosecutors, but not yet indicted, he went around the White House explaining why he wasn't guilty of the particular charges he faced. After he was indicted, he took a closer look at his position in light of his newfound Christian faith. Technically, he was right about his indictment, but he decided he was guilty of another violation. Colson walked in to the prosecutors and told them he couldn't plead guilty under the current indictment but was guilty of another crime. He said if they wanted to charge him with that offense, he would plead guilty. His ministry was born in prison.

Another caution is that the language of repentance can overlap with the language of confessions in the criminal justice context. Not every sin is a crime. Most sins are not crimes. Be careful that guilt due to sin does not make you think that you have done more than you actually have.

Phrases like "I'm sorry" are highly freighted with meaning. You are not in a forgiving situation, and your words, if it is necessary to speak now, should be chosen and delivered with extreme care. During my crisis, I cringed when I read my words, "I am at the same time sinking morally. I used to be able to put everything in perspective." Instead of reading the comment as the proactive worry about possible spiritual deadness that it was, a prosecutor might have tried to twist it into an admission that I had gone "over the line" into criminality. Of course, it was no such thing, but it underscores the warning that anything you say can and will be used against you.

Here is a beautiful paradox: as you draw closer to God, your deficiencies become more unacceptable to you. After Job, an Old Testament character who was "blameless and upright," talked directly to God, he said, "I had heard of you [the Lord] by the hearing of the ear, but now my eye sees you; therefore I despise myself, and repent in dust and ashes." This is part of the process of cleansing and obtaining "a new heart and a new spirit."

eleven

Self-Pity

From the ends of the earth we hear songs of praise, of glory to the Righteous One. But I say, I pine away, I pine away. Woe is me! For the treacherous deal treacherously, the treacherous deal very treacherously. (Isaiah 24:16)

One day, in the spring before I went to trial, I was talking to my wife. Actually, I was feeling sorry for myself and I was blubbering. After listening patiently to this, she said, "Quit sniveling!" She did not have to tell me twice. A few weeks later, for Father's Day, she got me a coffee mug that said, "Thou Shalt Not Snivel." I took it with me to trial that fall and drank deeply from it.

I had to separate self-pity from a couple of other emotional issues I was facing. The first was grief. I lost things that were very important to me, and those losses were permanent. The second was depression. Underneath my anger was profound sadness. Grief, anger, and sadness are legitimate. My self-pity, on the other hand, was a self-indulgent dwelling on my suffering.

The phrase "pity party" captures the practical problem with self-pity. My family and lawyers needed my focus on the task at hand – my defense – and I was constantly tempted to go off into a reverie of despair, as if no one as good as me had ever been here before. It is an excuse for inaction. That is the problem.

Grief can be worked through now or later. There are many stories of persons putting aside personal issues to deal with the task at hand.

Grief can usually wait. Mine was still there when I had time to deal with it. God is amply able to handle grief. The Psalmist marveled, "It is my grief that the right hand of the Most High has changed." Jesus taught, "Blessed are those who mourn, for they will be comforted."

Self-pity can either accompany or be an expression of depression. Depression has an additional physiological component. If depression threatens to overwhelm you and your personal resources are not enough, talk to your doctor. I was told that I was clinically depressed. That surprised me. I thought I was just having a normal response to an objectively awful situation. I understood that antidepression drugs could significantly flatten the patient's perceptions, and I decided against using them, based on my symptoms. Depression can be so deep that it severely alters the patient's understanding and undermines his or her ability to cope. If depression is your issue, you will need to make your own decision. In any event self-pity will not help.

President Richard Nixon struggled to pull himself out of periods of self-pity. He famously said, "No one is finished – until he quits."

A person of faith views loss, suffering, and adversity as schooling. The priest Henri Nouwen wrote, "Whatever happens – good things or bad, pleasant or problematic – we look and ask, 'What might God be doing here?' We see the events of the day as continuing occasions to change the heart."

Jesus ran into a man who had quit. It was at a pool in Jerusalem called Bethesda, reputed to have healing properties for the first person who got in it when it started to bubble. Invalids gathered there hoping to be healed by the bubbling waters. "One man was there who had been ill for thirty-eight years. When Jesus saw him lying there and knew that he had been there a long time, he said to him, 'Do you want to be made well?'"

The man started in with the self-pity. "The sick man answered him, 'Sir, I have no one to put me in the pool when the water is stirred up; and while I am making my way, someone else steps down ahead of me.'" The sick man didn't answer the question about whether he wanted to be made well, and Jesus didn't address the injustice the sick man raised. Instead, "Jesus said to him, 'Stand up, take your mat and walk.'"

Do you want to be made well? I will admit that there is a certain perverse pleasure in imagining that you are suffering like no other. It feeds the ego, which is otherwise starved in this time of accusation.

Reflecting on "What might God be doing here?" speaks no less to your importance. After all, God delights in you. What should you do in response?

Stand up, take your mat, and walk.

twelve

Suicide and the Will to Live

For the enemy has pursued me, crushing my life to the ground, making me sit in darkness like those long dead. Therefore my spirit faints within me; my heart within me is appalled. (Psalm 143:3–4)

Enron was once the seventh largest company in the world, according to *Fortune* magazine. Its leader Kenneth Lay had been heralded for his business insight and was the friend of US presidents. In 2001 Enron's stock plummeted, and by the end of the year, Enron was bankrupt. In the following years, numerous indictments, guilty pleas, and convictions followed.

In the spring of 2006, Mr. Lay was convicted of multiple counts of fraud by a federal jury in Houston, Texas. That summer, while awaiting sentencing, Lay, sixty-four, died of a heart attack. It was quite a surprise, and to many who hoped he would rot in prison, it was a bitter disappointment. The judge abated or set aside Mr. Lay's conviction.

Criminal law concerns itself only with the living. I found out that summer that if a defendant dies before sentencing, even if he was convicted, the indictment is dismissed and any conviction is abated or rendered void and of no effect. Such was my state of abandonment, betrayal, and fear that I went to the statute books and confirmed this information. According to the law, my death would even "solve" my Securities and Exchange Commission lawsuit.

It was like that moment in Frank Capra's classic movie *It's a Wonderful Life* when the evil manipulator Mr. Potter tells the falsely accused George Bailey, "You're worth more dead than alive." For a dangerously long time, George Bailey takes this statement to heart and goes to the brink of suicide.

An indictment changes the life of the accused forever. Whatever happened next, the "egg" that was my reputation had been scrambled and could not be unscrambled. It was natural to think, *My life is over.* I heard that some of my former coworkers said that when I was summarily and publicly fired, it was like I had died. Obviously, I had *not* died, and my life was *not* over. I had many choices left open, and my family needed *me* more than they needed my money or my so-called reputation.

Fyodor Dostoevsky was twenty-eight years old when he was led out to be executed for crimes against the czar. Terror filled him as he readied himself to die. At the last minute, his sentence was commuted to four years in prison in Siberia. He never forgot that day and forever afterward celebrated the desire to live one more minute. In Dostoevsky's masterpiece *Crime and Punishment*, Raskolnikov considers the saintly Sonya who became a prostitute to support her half brothers and sisters, who in return despised her. "But he fully understood the monstrous pain she suffered, and had long been suffering, at the thought of her dishonorable and shameful position. What, he wondered, what could so far have kept her from deciding to end it all at once?"

What could have kept her from deciding to end it all at once? Sonya was a marvel and transforming inspiration to Raskolnikov.

Sometime before trial, I was sitting alone at a coffee shop waiting for my daughter. Suddenly, my heart started beating irregularly. I thought for a moment about what might be happening. *The start of a heart attack?* In that moment I didn't care a bit about Kenneth Lay, abatement, prison, or my reputation. I turned away and prayed, like George Bailey, "I want to live! I want to live!"

So do you.

thirteen

Suicide in the Light of Faith, Reason, and Relationship

But he himself went a day's journey into the wilderness, and came and sat down under a solitary broom tree. He asked that he might die· "It is enough; now, O LORD, take away my life, for I am no better than my ancestors." (1 Kings 19:4)

In my community, we have suffered many suicides in the last several years. My family and I have lost neighbors and very close friends to suicide. I have seen and felt the devastation that follows. It continues for years and has not gone away. This made me very sensitive, going into this crisis, about the issue of suicide. When thoughts of death's possible advantages would come to my mind after the accusation, I was very alert to what I was doing with those thoughts. I became attentive to what was said by others about suicide.

Those who commit suicide often indicate that they see self-destruction as their only remaining choice. On the other hand, professional counselors often say suicide is a permanent solution to what is usually a temporary problem. The key to survival is to keep the other solutions in mind. It helps to know that you are not alone.

God sent Elijah to the northern Kingdom of Israel to warn against the idolatry of King Ahab and his wife, Jezebel. Elijah hosted a contest between the God of Israel and Jezebel's 450 false prophets. At the end of the contest, in which the false prophets and their gods were decisively vanquished, Queen Jezebel issued a death sentence against Elijah. Elijah skipped the jurisdiction and fled into the wilderness. At the end of the first day, Elijah "sat down under a solitary broom tree. He asked that he might die: 'It is enough; now, O LORD, take away my life, for I am no better than my ancestors.'"

I understand exactly how Elijah felt. I would wake up in the morning and realize (again) that my situation was not a nightmare arising from subconscious anxieties; it was a frightening and seemingly inexorable reality. On Sunday the preacher sometimes said, "Wake up every morning and thank God for another day." At that point in my life, that sometimes sounded like the taunt of an idiot.

Let's consider Elijah's request to die. There is a difference between the desire to cease living and a resolution "to end it all at once," in Dostoevsky's words. In the latter case, you move from abstract despair to very concrete thoughts – the current word is "ideation" – about how, when, and where you would kill yourself and what, if anything, you would say in the suicide note. If you are here, **get help now**! A switch has flipped in your mind, and there are prescription drugs that can calm you down sufficiently so you can start thinking clearly again.

You sometimes hear, usually at funerals for suicides, that they were mentally ill and didn't have much of a choice in the matter. There may be some cases where that is true. On the other hand, the great composer Ludwig van Beethoven told a friend, "If I had not read somewhere that a man should not voluntarily quit this life so long as he can still perform a good deed, I would have left this earth long ago – and, what is more, by my own hand."

Given that, you should carefully work through your reasoning on this issue. Here are a few things that you, like Beethoven, should take with you if you find yourself in a dark room considering suicide:

- You are not at the mercy of uncontrollable urges. You probably weren't suicidal before the accusation, so your fear and anxiety is a response to a new reality that you weren't prepared for. If you are at the ideation phase, call your doctor and ice down your mind.

- You always have another choice. By definition, if you continue to live, you have at least two choices. Something could happen tomorrow and give you a third and fourth choice. Torture survivor Jean Améry wrote, "Nothing really happens as we hope it will, nor as we fear it will."
- Committing suicide can be taken as confirmation of your guilt. Don't give your accusers the satisfaction. The gritty determination not to give up is a victory in itself, no matter how things turn out.
- You may believe you are a burden to your loved ones and suicide will relieve the burden. This is a treacherous bit of self-pity. There are not many survivors of a loved one's suicide who are grateful that their loved one took this action. More commonly, suicide leaves great and lasting devastation for the survivors. This can reverberate for generations.
- If everything goes wrong and you end up in prison and bankrupt, you will be in a position that literally millions before you have been in and survived. Your worst-case scenario is better than suicide.

At no point are you alone. God loves you and delights in you. Elijah wisely brought the matter directly to God. God had more for Elijah to do. We will talk about that in the next Meditation. There may be a purpose for good and an opportunity in this ordeal that only God knows. There is always hope.

It takes some effort to get out of bed in times like these. It can take a while to remember that "this is the day that the LORD has made." But it is.

fourteen

Suicide and the Example of Jesus

He was despised and rejected by others; a man of
suffering and acquainted with infirmity. (Isaiah 53:3)

After being sentenced to death by the queen, the prophet Elijah fled into the wilderness. Lonely and afraid, the fugitive wished to die. He had two choices – he could have turned this wish inward against himself, or he could have taken his wish to God.

After Elijah turned to God, he went to sleep. Twice, an angel came to him with fresh hot bread and cool water and told Elijah to eat. "He got up, and ate and drank; then he went in the strength of that food forty days and forty nights to Horeb the mount of God." Horeb is also known as Mt. Sinai, where Moses got the Ten Commandments.

Those meals from God – were they a dream? – sustained Elijah for "forty days and forty nights." Time is relative from a psychological perspective. Some events are so engaging that they are over before you know it. Some days never seem to end. Both things can happen at once. I read that one prisoner felt like every single day would never end, but he would always get to the end of the week and be shocked that seven days had passed so quickly.

We want so badly to fix the situation we are in. We want it now! Some desperately turn to thoughts of suicide as a solution. The story of Elijah reminds us that God will sustain us in the most extreme situations.

My troubles with the government ended thirty-three months after they started. During that time, I was blessed to live in Dallas County, Texas. In November 2006 we elected a district attorney who decided to pay attention to the claims of some convicts who maintained their innocence. Every few months following my indictment, there would be a new story of a local man freed after decades in prison for a crime that he did not commit. The DNA technology that led to these men being set free was discovered years after their conviction. It wasn't faith in humanity that sustained them in prison, sometimes on death row. To a person, they were sustained by faith in God and the example of Jesus.

Most people look at Jesus a certain way. The accused have a whole other insight into Jesus. All Christians look at Jesus as "the pioneer and perfecter of our faith." The accused have a visceral reaction to the rest of this verse and the next verse, where we are reminded that "for the sake of the joy that was set before him [Jesus] endured the cross, disregarding its shame...Consider him who endured such hostility against himself from sinners, so that you may not grow weary or lose heart." Jesus suffered shame, hostility, weariness, and the temptation to despair. I was electrified when I first read these verses after my indictment.

Here is a God who understands. Here is a God who gets it. This is a God worth talking to – a God who has the credibility to say to me, "Endure trials for the sake of discipline. God is treating you as children; for what child is there whom a parent does not discipline?"

On the forty-first day of Elijah's escape into the wilderness, the LORD came to Mount Horeb and asked, "What are you doing here, Elijah?"

Elijah spilled forth his sadness tinged with more than a little self-pity. Without expressing any judgment, God asked Elijah to go stand outside the cave in which he was hiding, "for the LORD is about to pass by." After a great show, God quietly gave Elijah some important things he needed to do for God. These tasks required that Elijah return to the queen's jurisdiction.

When Elijah completed these tasks, he ascended into heaven in a chariot of fire. Ironically, the man who once despaired and asked that he might die left the earth without ever tasting death.

Preserve your choices. Trust in the LORD. "[R]un with perseverance the race that is set before [you.]"

fifteen

Sought Out

[A]n angel of the Lord appeared to him in a dream and said, "Joseph, son of David, do not be afraid to take Mary as your wife, for the child conceived in her is from the Holy Spirit. She will bear a son, and you are to name him Jesus, for he will save his people from their sins." All this took place to fulfill what had been spoken by the Lord through the prophet: "Look, the virgin shall conceive and bear a son, and they shall name him Emmanuel," which means, "God is with us." (Matthew 1:20–23)

I found myself accused and ostracized. Nothing had prepared me for this. I began to look around for role models.

It occurred to me one day to look at the story of Joseph, of "coat of many colors" fame. Joseph, his father, and his brothers lived in the land of Canaan in the early second millennium BC. Out of jealousy, Joseph's brothers sold him into slavery in Egypt. An Egyptian named Potiphar, an officer of Pharaoh, bought Joseph and made him the overseer of his household. Joseph was handsome and good-looking, and Potiphar's wife was restless.

Potiphar's wife falsely accused Joseph of attempted rape. They were in the house alone. She had some of his clothes. It was her word against his, and he was a slave and a foreigner. Potiphar was enraged and threw Joseph in prison.

As a teenager I learned about Joseph's exemplary behavior resisting the sexual temptations offered by Potiphar's wife. There wasn't much discussion in the church youth group about Joseph's time in prison.

I reread the story in chapter 39 of Genesis. Joseph "remained there in prison." In fact, he remained there for years, forgotten.

I was delighted and challenged by what was written next. The scripture says, "But the LORD was with Joseph and showed him steadfast love." The chief jailer came to trust Joseph, and he put him in charge of the other prisoners. "The chief jailer paid no heed to anything that was in Joseph's care, because the LORD was with him; and whatever he did, the LORD made it prosper."

The LORD was with him!

I was notified that I was a "target" just before Advent, the four-week period when Christians contemplate the coming of Jesus on Christmas day. Years earlier, a former federal prosecutor explained to me that a "target" is a person on whose neck the "jackboot of the government" was firmly and permanently planted.

During Advent 2006 the scripture about Jesus being "'Emmanuel,' which means 'God is with us'" and the Christmas carol "O Come, O Come, Emmanuel" helped deepen the message that I found in the story of Joseph.

God was with Joseph, "God is with us," but was God with me?

In the New Year, I prayed for God to be with me and for God to be with the prosecutor working on the indictment. On the day I pled "not guilty," I had an experience that assured me that God was with me, too. God sought me out. That evening, alone in a second-rate hotel and thousands of miles from home, I became profoundly aware that God knew my troubles. At my trial I picked a spot in the courtroom to look at whenever I needed to remind myself that God was there.

I never knew until my verdict was read what God had in mind for me, but I was always comforted by the example of the LORD's steadfast love for Joseph.

After my government troubles were over, I was with a church team visiting a jail. We were in one pod with about twenty prisoners. Only two or three came out to the tables to talk to us. The rest seemed uninterested or were wrapped in blankets in their bunks, apparently sleeping. I started to talk to one fellow about God being with Joseph when he was in prison. From a bunk in the corner, a voice called out, "Joseph was innocent too!"

God seeks each of us out. Even the accused. Especially the accused.

sixteen

Touching Bottom

In my distress I called upon the L○RD; to my God I cried for help. From his temple he heard my voice, and my cry to him reached his ears…The L○RD also thundered in the heavens, and the Most High uttered his voice. And he sent down his arrows, and scattered them; he flashed forth lightnings, and routed them…He reached down from on high, he took me; he drew me out of mighty waters. He delivered me from my strong enemy, and from those who hated me; for they were too mighty for me. They confronted me in the day of my calamity; but the L○RD was my support. He brought me out into a broad place; he delivered me, because he delighted in me. (Psalm 18:6, 13-14, 16-19)

I have written favorably about my church. However, church members and clergy are quite capable of reinforcing the dislocation, abandonment, and rejection of the accused. My church is filled with members who love "law and order," especially order. One day I wandered into a Sunday school class learning about 1 Peter 4:12 – 19. My ears perked up when the teacher talked about the apostle Peter's injunction to "rejoice insofar as you are sharing Christ's sufferings."

My hope for a little direct encouragement was dashed when the teacher emphasized the part of Peter's letter that said, "But let none of you suffer as a murderer, a thief, a criminal or even as a mischief maker" (verse 15). The Sunday school teacher made clear his highly educated view that one accused of being a criminal was outside the promise of this scripture. He seemed incapable of understanding that one could "suffer as a...thief" and not be a thief. Clearly, he had missed the part of the Gospels where Jesus "suffered as a" blasphemer and insurrectionist, though he was neither.

That day, I went home and started to have a bad Sunday afternoon. I had mistaken the teacher's highly erudite but wrong views for the views of the church. It is a common mistake, but I was struggling with the church's implied disapproval.

Where did I fit in God's view? I drew on what I had been taught and experienced to create a personal affirmation of faith. I decided that I believe the following:

- God loves me.
- God is with me.
- God will strengthen me.
- Trust in the LORD.
- Prayer works.
- What others intend for evil, God can make work for good.

A few weeks later, my wife was studying Psalm 18. Reading it, I realized that my affirmation that "God loves me" didn't quite capture the whole truth. The Psalmist declared that the LORD "delivered me, because he delighted in me."

After weeks of sinking, I felt myself finally touch bottom. The image of God "delighting" in me was firm ground. I was miles from the surface – let alone the safety of the shore – but I had a foothold to resist the "mighty waters" into which I had been thrown. "The LORD sits enthroned over the flood."

In the novel *Dead Souls*, Gogol asks, "For what is the significance of the fact that even in his degradation, a man besmirched and going to his ruin claims still to be loved?" What is the significance, indeed? The best Gogol comes up with is that it is "the faint cry of a soul stifled." It looks to me more like the hopeful cry of a soul responding to the presence of God.

God doesn't just love you; God delights in you. God's love is strength for the journey. No matter where you are in this mess, you are in good company.

seventeen

What is Humility?

Humble yourselves therefore under the mighty hand of God, so that he may exalt you in due time. Cast all your anxiety on him, because he cares for you. Discipline yourselves, keep alert. Like a roaring lion your adversary the devil prowls around, looking for someone to devour. Resist him, steadfast in your faith, for you know that your brothers and sisters in all the world are undergoing the same kinds of suffering. And after you have suffered for a little while, the God of all grace, who has called you to his eternal glory in Christ, will himself restore, support, strengthen, and establish you. To him be the power, forever and ever. Amen. (1 Peter 5:6–11)

After I was indicted, a friend of mine who worked in the Department of Justice recommended that I read a recent study analyzing how people best cope with natural and man-made disasters, such as avalanches and shipwrecks. The author of the study concludes, "To experience humility is the true survivor's correct response to catastrophe."

In the end, the answer to the problems of the accused is humility. The questions are, what is humility and what behaviors and attitudes does humility consist of?

The Bible is filled with answers to these questions. For me personally, the most relevant example of humility is King Hezekiah of Judah, who reigned from 715 BC to 686 BC. "He did what was right in the sight of the LORD just as his ancestor David had done. [T]here was no one like him among all the kings of Judah after him, or among those who were before him...The LORD was with him."

Hezekiah reigned during the time of the Assyrian empire. The Assyrians were the world's first superpower. Their innovations in chariot technology made them invincible militarily. In those days people believed that territories were protected by specific local gods. Wise diplomacy required that the gods of neighboring territories be worshipped so they would provide a buffer against more powerful enemies. This is the source of the idolatry that persisted throughout the Old Testament. Hezekiah's father met the king of Assyria face to face and decided to begin fervent worship of the god of Damascus, which was located between Judah and Assyria.

Throwing his father's prudence to the wind, Hezekiah instead rooted out all forms of idolatry from Judah and refused to pay further tribute to the empire. "For he held fast to the LORD; he did not depart from following him but kept the commandments that the LORD commanded Moses."

Assyria's response was swift. It sent a massive army to besiege Jerusalem. At the walls of Jerusalem, the Assyrian spokesman taunted the Jews for their faith in God, saying, "Has any of the gods of the nations ever delivered its land out of the hand of the king of Assyria?"

Hezekiah had many options, but he considered only one. He "covered himself with sackcloth, and went into the house of the LORD." He prayed, "This day is a day of distress, of rebuke, of disgrace; children have come to the birth, and there is no strength to bring them forth." The reference to children may not make immediate sense to a man, but a mother will get it. Once a woman goes into labor – the child has "come to the birth" – she has no real say in whether the child will be born. Her body takes over. Whether she is weak or strong, the child will be born. Hezekiah thus gracefully acknowledged that he was powerless and was completely dependent on the LORD.

This insight freed Hezekiah and the people of Jerusalem to rely on the LORD fully.

The people of Jerusalem went to bed that night having no objective reason to doubt that they would be destroyed in the morning.

The humility of Hezekiah consisted in this: "He trusted in the LORD." Humility is not knowing and still trusting fully in the LORD. This is the proper attitude of the humble. This is what a humble person does.

The accused is familiar with this uncomfortable feeling of powerlessness and dependence. Through a series of shocks, I realized I had no control over important aspects of my life. People would think what they would think, say what they would say, stack the decks how they wanted them stacked, and there was nothing I could do about it.

In the weeks just before I was indicted, my lawyer would forward me facsimile transmissions from the prosecutor, and I would hide in my bathroom and cry until I got the courage to read them. I looked at one of the faxes and realized one of the attached documents was a transparent forgery, and the other said the opposite of what the prosecutor said it showed. *Surely this will change his mind*, I thought. Nevertheless, I was indicted.

In the months that followed, I sat in depositions aware that untrue testimony could sink me. My wife sat home in terrified silence until I could call her after each and reassure her that "I still have all my fingers and toes."

I knew I had no control, but I knew and felt that God was there. Things that I feared could go wrong did not.

In a gradual process of revelation, I started looking around at other things I could not control and began to see the blessing. I had no control over any of the accidents of my birth and upbringing – that I was born, at this time, in this country, under these laws, to these parents, with this set of talents. These things were given to me. I was drawn to notice more fundamental gifts that I had no control over – the extravagance of nature, the transmission of wisdom, the kindness of strangers, the deep character of my wife, and the witness of the scriptures.

I knew God created and provided all of these wonderful advantages. The German theologian Rudolph Otto said there is a point where a person – if he is paying attention – becomes deeply aware that God created him. It is a moment of awe and sometimes fear. In the Old Testament, fear and awe are synonymous. The Book of Proverbs says, "The fear of the LORD is the beginning of knowledge." This insight arises when we see beyond what we can control to what we can't. Being accused was the first time I looked beyond what I could control. There was a wordless wonder that hit me when it fully dawned on me that I am God's creation.

This profound sense of being God's creature, abundantly provisioned by God, makes trusting in the LORD the most natural thing in the world. There is a parable of Jesus that I had never noticed before this. Jesus said, "The kingdom of God is as if someone would scatter seed on the ground, and would sleep and rise night and day, and the seed would sprout and grow, he does not know how. The earth produces of itself, first the stalk, then the head, then the full grain of the head. But when the grain is ripe, at once he goes in with his sickle, because the harvest has come."

That's the thing about trusting in the LORD. It works for the seed scatterer, but he or she does not know how. In Hezekiah's case God acted to change the situation. "That very night the angel of the LORD set out and struck down one hundred eighty-five thousand in the camp of the Assyrians; when the morning dawned, they were all dead bodies. Then King Sennacherib of Assyria left [and] went home."

The army arrayed against an accused person is awesomely powerful. I was up against "the world's last superpower." However, the powers of this world are subject to God.

eighteen
Humility and Anxiety

They went to a place called Gethsemane...And going a little farther, he threw himself on the ground and prayed that, if it were possible, the hour might pass from him. He said, "Abba, Father, for you all things are possible; remove this cup from me; yet, not what I want, but what you want." (Mark 14:32, 35–36)

After being designated as a federal target, I needed to talk to someone who had gone through this and come out the other end. A man in my church agreed to talk to me. It was a brief visit filled with wonderful insight. He said what constantly guided him through his troubles was the part of the LORD's Prayer that said, "Thy will be done." It took me a while to digest that observation.

If you don't trust in the LORD, where do you put your faith? In Old Testament times, people would pray to a variety of gods – this one for better crops, that one for more children, another one to keep away enemies. These gods would be worshiped alongside the true God so as to keep all of the cosmos happy.

Elijah was called to bring the northern kingdom back to God. He hosted a great meeting of the people of Israel and invited the 450 false prophets of Queen Jezebel. He shouted to the assembled Israelites, "How long will you go limping with two different opinions? If the LORD is God, follow him; but if Baal, follow him." (We have already discussed how this meeting turned out.)

Elijah's phrase "go limping with" is wonderfully meaningful. It suggests an action that is intended to improve performance but actually hobbles the performer instead. As we know from history, idolatry was not a successful strategy for the Israelites. In more modern times, idolatry is identified with greed and the love of money and the things money can buy, such as prestige and status. Experience shows that you really can't have enough money, prestige, or status if you are trying to trust in it.

My personal "idol" had been my resume, as silly as that sounds. I worked tirelessly to build a body of accomplishment that I hoped would secure my position in the corporate world for years to come. My list of titles was impressive and growing. I created successful programs – models to be emulated – and improved the quality of my department without increasing its size. I had been on national and international television and was quoted in newspapers. I wrote articles and made speeches – a very significant one was scheduled for the week I was fired. It never seemed to be enough. I spent too much time improving my resume, literally flying around the world in search of the career achievement that would finally calm my anxiety. My quest was just as ridiculous as praying to a stone statue.

After I was fired, I took another look at my resume, which I knew had been helpfully provided to the government. I immediately saw the irony. It wasn't wrong for me to do a good job. It was wrong for me to put my faith in it. I sensed that my career as a corporate executive was over, notwithstanding all my hard work. I also knew that in the coming months, my accusers would misuse all those titles, programs, and skills and try to hang them around my neck like a millstone. My decades-long creeping fear that my resume would never do for me what I wanted it to do was confirmed. I could finally see that my anxiety had been a direct result of relying on an idol for security.

Jesus taught that, in reality, you cannot "go limping" between trusting God and your personal idols. He said, "No one can serve two masters; for a slave will either hate the one and love the other, or be devoted to the one and despise the other. You cannot serve God and wealth."

The apostle Peter explained the reason for trusting in the LORD for your security. He said, "Cast all your anxiety on [God], because he cares for you." If God cares for me, I can be confident in asking that God's will be done.

Resolving, like my friend, to trust wholly in God and ask that God's will be done may seem crazy at first blush, but in the final analysis, the LORD is wholly trustworthy. Even as society condemns and turns its back on the accused, God still cares for you. Gather up all of your personal idols and throw them away. Trusting in the LORD is the only reliable choice.

nineteen

Cultivating Humility

There is none like you among the gods, O Lᴏʀᴅ, nor are there any works
like yours. All the nations you have made shall come and bow down
before you, O Lᴏʀᴅ, and shall glorify your name. For you are great
and do wondrous things; you alone are God. (Psalm 86:8–10)

In a catastrophe, a person's illusions of control are stripped away. For
many this is a blessing, a very well-disguised blessing.

Humility is the result of an accurate understanding of God's relationship to you as God's creation. The Psalmist said, God "delivered me,
because he delighted in me." Peter said, God "cares for you."

I think a human's comprehension of his or her relationship with God
is itself a gift from God. God must seek us out for us to be enlightened.
God has most certainly sought us out through Jesus and the scriptures
and, in a more intimate way, through loved ones and the Holy Spirit.

Once obtained, humility and trust in the Lᴏʀᴅ can be nurtured.
Here are some exercises that I found useful:

First, keep in mind the relative sizes of things. The accusation
against you and both its likely and potential result should not be considered solely in light of your own resources. You should keep in mind
the scope of God's ability to get things done.

Second, count your blessings. Notwithstanding the accusation, you
are richly blessed. My grocery checker kept telling me, "I'm just glad

the Lord let me wake up on this side of the dirt this morning." Amen. There is a chipper little song that I sang as a child that came back to me again and again during my troubles.

> When upon life's billows you are tempest-tossed,
> When you are discouraged, thinking all is lost,
> Count your many blessings;
> Name them one by one,
> And it will surprise you what the Lord has done...
> So amid the conflict, whether great or small,
> Do not be discouraged; God is over all.
> Count your many blessings,
> Angels will attend,
> Help and comfort give you to your journey's end.

Third, recall how God has acted in the past. Jews and Christians constantly recite the many ways God has sustained them. The Jews celebrate their deliverance from captivity in the Passover meal. Christians celebrate the death and resurrection of Jesus in the Lord's Supper. The remembrance of these events encourages trust in the Lord.

Fourth, be aware that God's purposes may be very different from what you think you need. Let's be blunt: Just because a person is innocent doesn't mean he or she won't go to prison. It was certainly a great injustice that Alexander Solzhenitsyn was imprisoned. However, who can read *The Gulag Archipelago*, his magnificent expose of Soviet inhumanity, and not thank God? The apostle Paul wrote, "I want you to know, beloved, that what has happened to me has actually helped to spread the gospel, so that it has become known throughout the entire imperial guard and to everyone else that my imprisonment is for Christ; and most of the brothers and sisters, having been made confident in the Lord by my imprisonment, dare to speak the word with greater boldness and without fear."

Fifth, be ready to do what God says. After Judah's great deliverance from the Assyrians during the time of King Hezekiah, the Jews came to believe that their kingdom would always be preserved. One hundred years later, the Babylonians threatened Judah. God sent the prophet Jeremiah to tell them the kingdom was finished and they should go to Babylon. The Jews did not want to hear what God was saying. They attacked the messenger. Jeremiah was labeled a traitor and imprisoned. The prophecy was true, and many of the people were taken as captives to Babylon. However, it was actually a blessing. God knew what the children of Israel needed better than they did. The Jews who went into the Babylonian captivity were renewed and sustained through the faithfulness of God and his servants Ezekiel, Nehemiah, Ezra, and Daniel.

Sixth, get right with God. You may not be guilty of the accusation against you. That does not mean that you have not, in some other way, "sinned and fallen short of the glory of God." A closer relationship with God will bring these sins more painfully to the surface. This is a very good time to repent and ask for God's forgiveness.

Seventh, be willing to wait for the LORD. The Psalmist said, "Wait for the LORD; be strong, and let your heart take courage; wait for the LORD!" Our society has a bias toward action. We tend to jump frantically about. Patience is called for. Facing indictment, you are in quicksand, and purposeless movement can just sink you in deeper.

twenty

Humility is Active

But the Israelites broke faith in regard to the devoted things... and the anger of the Lord burned against the Israelites... So about three thousand of the people went up there [to Ai]; and they fled before the men of Ai. The men of Ai killed about thirty-six of them, chasing them from outside the gate as far as Shebarim and killing them on the slope. The hearts of the people melted and turned to water. Then Joshua tore his clothes, and fell to the ground on his face before the ark of the Lord until the evening, he and the elders of Israel; and they put dust on their heads. Joshua said, "Ah, Lord God! Why have you brought this people across the Jordan at all, to hand us over to the Amorites so as to destroy us? Would that we had been content to settle beyond the Jordan! O Lord, what can I say, now that Israel has turned their backs to their enemies! The Canaanites and all the inhabitants of the land will hear of it, and surround us, and cut off our name from the earth. Then what will you do for your great name?" The Lord said to Joshua, "Stand up! Why have you fallen upon your face?" (Joshua 7:1, 4–10)

An early piece of advice that I received was to keep my chin up. In certain very dark times, I needed to remind myself of the stronger version of "chin up" that the Lord gave to Joshua after his first defeat in the conquest of Canaan. The Lord said to the prostrate Joshua, "Stand up! Why have you fallen upon your face?" Talk about a pep talk. Like Joshua, I was in a battle. I repeated that scripture to myself often, out loud, and with emphasis.

An aspect of humility is waiting for the LORD. This can be mistaken for passivity. Humility is not passive.

Once, a fellow was stranded on a leaky life raft in the ocean. He prayed that God would deliver him. As he was praying, a luxury yacht came by and asked if he needed anything. He brightly replied, "No, the LORD will provide." He faithfully waited. Finally, his life raft deflated and he drowned.

As he came to the Pearly Gates, St. Peter was confused. He said, "You aren't supposed to be here for many more years. What happened?"

The fellow said, "I prayed for deliverance, but it didn't come, and I drowned."

St. Peter was even more flustered, made a call to check on something, and finally he asked, "Didn't you see the yacht that God sent by for you?"

After my trial a man called me to talk about how to manage himself in his upcoming criminal trial. Shortly after the introductions, we said to each other, almost simultaneously, "At least we're not in China!" We were referring to the legal system. A businessman in China had just been executed there over some adulterated food.

It is a terrible thing being indicted, and it is a terrible thing awaiting trial, but in the United States, once you are indicted, you have finally stepped onto a playing field that has well-established rules and has a genuine, if imperfectly realized, aim of achieving justice and protecting the innocent. I became acquainted early with the statistic that the federal conviction rate is 92 percent. That was supposed to be daunting to me. I took it differently. Eight percent is at least a fighting chance. I suspected that the statistic included guilty pleas (of which there were a lot), so the chance for justice in a contested trial seemed like it might be much higher.

There is no reason for passivity. You have much to do with your family and your lawyers. Nothing about trial preparation is inconsistent with trusting in the LORD. The trial, the lawyers, the judge, the procedures, and the jury – these all may be the yacht that God has sent in response to your needs.

twenty-one
Responding

After I was indicted, I was able to look at the documents, witness statements, and other evidence forming the government's case against me. In the boxes of paper I received was a two-hundred-plus-page slide presentation that had been given to the prosecutors before they indicted me and sued me for securities fraud. It consisted of pictures of documents, such as corporate board minutes, e-mails, and contracts with my name or signature prominently highlighted in yellow everywhere it appeared. The stated goal of the presentation was to "Focus on Kent Roberts." Stripped as it was of context and enhanced by snippets of volunteered witness statements, the report was designed to create a terrible impression.

As I studied the tens of thousands of documents, I saw that a couple of key witnesses had their own paper trail that might be open to question. With this information I had an opportunity to put them in an uncomfortable situation. I thought about it hard. The immunity these men had been given was galling. If their actions were called out and made into a big issue, it could change the dynamic of my case. I certainly felt they deserved some pain.

In the end I reflected on my own distress, disappointment, and fear and concluded that I wouldn't wish this experience on my worst enemy – in this case, literally.

Jesus said, "In everything do to others as you would have them do to you; for this is the law and the prophets." This is called the Golden Rule. My parents told me, when I was a child, to follow the Golden Rule. To this sound advice, I will add – now more than ever.

Bad behavior is common in the context of an accusation. Bad behavior was directed at me. The temptation was strong to treat others the way I was being treated, not the way I wanted to be treated.

Follow the Golden Rule.

The opposite path is well marked. When I respond to bad behavior with bad behavior, my capacity to do the right thing is diminished. When I respond in kind, the bad behavior of the other person becomes the rationale for my actions. The worse my response, the more I need to build up the bitterness and accumulation of grievances to justify my actions. This type of thinking can twist me into knots, and I become compromised. If I keep at it, I will begin to dehumanize and demonize others.

Jesus said the Golden Rule "is the law and the prophets" – in other words, a summary of all God's teaching – because it is the practical embodiment of the commandment to "love one another." A major part of love is empathy, the ability to appreciate the feelings and position of another person. This is hard to do when the other person is trying to put you in prison. Still, we are called to love one another and have empathy. The Golden Rule provides a practical guide in this difficult situation.

Piper Kerman spent thirteen months in federal prison for transporting drug money. She had lived a privileged life and gone to one of the best schools. For an adventure Kerman got involved with a group that sold drugs. She didn't directly deal drugs, but she helped move the cash proceeds around. She never gave a thought to the effects of the drugs on their customers until she met many of them in prison. During her time inside, she became friends with many women whose lives were wrecked by drug abuse. For the first time, she saw what she had been doing. She concluded, "Lack of empathy lies at the heart of every crime – certainly my own."

You can make your situation worse by responding to bad behavior in kind. Why do that? You don't have to get down on the level of your accusers to stand up for yourself.

One day this will be over. This is what I will tell you about that day: You will want to look back at your own actions and reactions without regrets. You will want to disentangle yourself from the experience emotionally. You will want to be able to forgive. If you used the bad behavior of others to justify your own actions, you will be less free to forgive.

The beauty of the Golden Rule is that it is so easy to apply. I always know exactly how I want to be treated. I may or may not know why someone is treating me badly. They may not even think they are treating me badly. In truth they may not actually be treating me badly at all.

I can't always figure out their motives, but I can always understand the treatment I would like to receive. It is treatment that is kind and just and thoughtful. That is how I should treat others.

"Do to others as you would have them do to you." Now more than ever.

twenty-two
Silence

Now the chief priests and the whole council were looking for testimony against Jesus to put him to death; but they found none. For many gave false testimony against him, and their testimony did not agree. Some stood up and gave false testimony against him, saying, "We heard him say, 'I will destroy this temple that is made with hands, and in three days I will build another, not made with hands.'" But even on this point their testimony did not agree. Then the high priest stood up before them and asked Jesus, "Have you no answer? What is it that they testify against you?" But he was silent and did not answer. Again the high priest asked him, "Are you the Messiah, the Son of the Blessed One?" Jesus said, "I am; and 'you will see the Son of Man seated at the right hand of the Power,' and 'coming with the clouds of heaven.'" Then the high priest tore his clothes and said, "Why do we still need witnesses? You have heard his blasphemy! What is your decision?" All of them condemned him as deserving death. (Mark 14:55–64)

If the average person knows one thing about criminal law, it is that "you have the right to remain silent. Anything you say can and will be used against you." This is part of the *Miranda* warning that is to be given to a person who is taken into police custody.

Silence has enormous practical benefits. As Mark's account of the trial of Jesus portrays, anything you say can and will be twisted and then used against you. If your mouth is open, cooperating witnesses will be happy to fill it with whatever suits the need of the moment. The government uses this type of testimony because most crimes require evidence of malicious intent. This can be hard to come by if only objective facts, like the actual contemporaneous documents, are used.

Listening is an act of good faith, and good faith can be in short supply. Jeremiah prophesied during the final days of the Kingdom of Judah at the turn of the sixth century BC. The kingdom was under constant pressure from the Babylonian Empire. Jeremiah was spreading the word of the LORD that the kingdom would end and the people should permit themselves to be taken captive to Babylon, or Chaldea as it was sometimes known. The leaders of Judah viewed the prophecy proclaimed by Jeremiah as treason.

Once, when the siege was lifted, Jeremiah tried to leave Jerusalem to visit his homestead located in the territory of Benjamin, which was north of the city. The sentry at the Benjamin Gate stopped him, "saying, 'You are deserting to the Chaldeans.' And Jeremiah said, 'That is a lie; I am not deserting to the Chaldeans.' But Irijah [the sentry] would not listen to him, and arrested Jeremiah and brought him to the officials." Once he got there, Jeremiah wisely had nothing to say. "The officials were enraged at Jeremiah, and they beat him and they imprisoned him...many days." Once rage was involved, nothing Jeremiah actually said was going to be accurately recalled.

The benefits of silence dawned on me with crushing force when I first read the statements of the government witnesses. I was astonished. Fortunately for me, the witnesses couldn't agree with their own selves, let alone each other.

Remaining silent is very hard. Prior to the accusation, I trusted in the integrity of others and believed they would evaluate what I said fairly. I wanted to explain things. Even when things weren't going that well, I thought, *It's all a big misunderstanding. I can straighten this out.* It is a naïve view, but it is a natural instinct. The Psalmist described the struggle to keep silent: "I said, 'I will guard my ways that I may not sin with my tongue; I will keep a muzzle on my mouth as long as the wicked are in my presence.' I was silent and still; I held my peace to no avail; my distress grew worse, my heart became hot within me. While I mused, the fire burned."

The Christian writer Thomas á Kempis underscored the spiritual aspect of the decision to remain silent. He wrote a series of imagined dialogues between Jesus and a faithful person. In one, Jesus says, "A wise man remains silent when beset by evil; he turns to Me in his heart, and is untroubled by man's judgments. Do not let your peace depend on what people say of you, for whether they speak good or ill of you makes no difference to what you are." Beyond the practical benefit of silence, á Kempis says, are profound questions: Whose opinion matters to you? Who are you trying to please?

There will be a day when, one way or the other, the time of troubles will be over for the accused. That will be a day for rejoicing, loud and vocal rejoicing! The Psalmist describes how that day will feel: "I waited patiently for the LORD; he inclined to me and heard my cry. He drew me up from the desolate pit, out of the miry bog, and set my feet upon a rock, making my steps secure. He put a new song in my mouth, a song of praise to our God. Many will see and fear, and put their trust in the LORD."

Wait patiently. The day for speaking will come.

twenty-three

Hoping and Waiting

I believe that I shall see the goodness of the Lᴏʀᴅ in the land
of the living. Wait for the Lᴏʀᴅ; be strong, and let your heart
take courage; wait for the Lᴏʀᴅ! (Psalm 27:13–14)

During my troubles, I often had a nagging sense that I should be doing
something more, but I didn't know what it was, and I had this tremendous fear that whatever I did would go wrong and send me to prison.
It was not simply that I was operating in a context with which I had
no experience. I lost confidence in my ability to understand or predict
anything. These are probably the main job skills of a lawyer if you think
about it. How could my understanding be so far off? If my judgment
was off then, as my accusers claimed, how can I make a decision now?

Compounding this was a distinct understanding that I was in "sud-
den-death overtime." One mistake could seal my fate. I heard stories
about how jurors seized on one grimace the defendant made to decide
on a guilty verdict. My family and I were monitoring my face to make
sure none of the pain I was feeling was reflected on it. This was its own
source of unhappiness.

I discovered the word "disquiet," which expressed this agitated
state of dissatisfaction with inaction coupled with a paralyzing fear of
movement. Right after I discovered the word, I read Psalm 42, which
asks, "Why are you cast down, O my soul, and why are you disquieted

within me?" The Psalmist answers, "Hope in God; for I shall again praise him, my help and my God."

Hope has a vivid meaning for me. When I was six or seven, my mother had the job of teaching the younger children the songs of the church. There was a very popular anthem in our church that had a second verse that the congregation, and certainly the children, did not sing very often. Mom taught us that second verse.

> When dark clouds of trouble hang o'er us
> And threaten our peace to destroy,
> There is hope smiling brightly before us,
> And we know that deliverance is nigh.
> We doubt not the Lord nor his goodness,
> We've proved him in days that are past.

To prompt us when we performed the song for the adults, Mom made a series of posters. She drew a large cartoon of the sun brightly shining with a ludicrous grinning face to help us remember the line about "hope smiling brightly." Four decades later, that cartoon and this verse came back to me clearly at critical times.

The logic of hope is a willingness to wait for the Lord. The Psalmist says, "Our soul waits for the Lord; he is our help and shield. Our heart is glad in him, because we trust in his holy name. Let your steadfast love, O Lord, be upon us, even as we hope in you."

Emma Whittemore was an important social worker who was active in New York City from 1890 to 1920. At the beginning of her work, she found herself stymied. She felt called to help the city's prostitutes and unwed mothers but could not figure out how best to do it. She wrote, "Not knowing just what to do, I was compelled to do nothing. That, after all, in most cases, is about the best position any Christian can occupy, for God can then have a chance to make known His will without any interference upon your part."

The idea of getting out of God's way is ancient. In another context the apostle Paul said, "Beloved, never avenge yourselves, but leave room for the wrath of God." Waiting hopefully leaves room for God to act.

The most useful Psalm for me during this time was Psalm 27. It ends with this affirmation: "I believe that I shall see the goodness of the LORD in the land of the living. Wait for the LORD; be strong, and let your heart take courage; wait for the LORD!" That became my prayer.

From the depths of trouble, Job asked, "[W]here then is my hope?"

My answer to Job's question was prepared by God through my Mom forty years before I needed it and stored away in the sweetest possible memory. "Hope smiling brightly" with a silly grin.

twenty-four

Loss

We are treated as imposters, and yet are true; as unknown, and yet are well known; as dying, and see – we are alive; as punished, and yet not killed; as sorrowful, yet always rejoicing; as poor, yet making many rich; as having nothing, and yet possessing everything. (2 Corinthians 6:8–10)

Years ago, I was privileged to pray with a group of devout Muslims. We were working together on a Habitat for Humanity house, and the prayer was to dedicate the day's work to God. Most of the Christians folded their hands in front of their body as they prayed. The Muslims held their hands in front of them cupped with the palms upward and the fingers loosely intertwined. It looked like an impromptu ladle.

Later, I asked my friend Marzuk about his prayer stance. "Is it so you can receive God's gifts?" I asked.

"Yes, that, and also, so that God can take what he wants from me," he replied.

That was a powerful and useful thought. After Job's life fell apart, he said, "Naked I came from my mother's womb, and naked shall I return there; the LORD gave, and the LORD has taken away; blessed be the name of the LORD."

The accused loses a lot. I knew that even if I was later exonerated, I was not going to be restored to where I was professionally or socially. On a simple matter like working, it is well known that the employment prospects of an ex-convict are poor. I read a study recently that examined whether those who become involved in the criminal justice system and are found not guilty do any better. There was no evidence that they did any better than convicts, and there was evidence that the taint of mere involvement with the system persists despite acquittal.

I experienced permanent loss. However, all was not lost.

I am not saying that this loss is caused by God but that God provides an opportunity in it. The writer of Ecclesiastes wrote, "Do not say, 'Why were the former days better than these?' For it is not wisdom that you ask this. Wisdom is as good as an inheritance, an advantage to those who see the sun. For the protection of wisdom is like the protection of money, and the advantage of knowledge is that wisdom gives life to the one who possesses it...In the day of prosperity be joyful, and in the day of adversity consider; God has made the one as well as the other."

There are some things that are important to lose. Bill Wilson, the founder of Alcoholics Anonymous, wrote, "Those adolescent urges that so many of us have for top approval, perfect security, and perfect romance – urges quite appropriate to age seventeen – prove to be an impossible way of life when we are at age forty-seven or fifty-seven."

On a mundane level, I lost fifteen pounds because I had time finally to eat and exercise properly. I lost the need – I'm not being sarcastic – to receive hundreds of e-mails and dozens of phone calls a day. I lost a lot of trust, illusions, and false dependencies.

It is human nature to resist profound change. Saul was the first king of Israel. When it came time to anoint him king, he couldn't be found. The LORD said, "See, he has hidden himself among the baggage." Saul had serious issues with fear and timidity. God did what God could to help Saul lose this. The prophet Samuel told Saul, "[T]he spirit of the LORD will possess you, and you will...be turned into a different person." "As he turned away to leave Samuel, God gave him another heart." The "heart transplant" was rejected. Saul never gave up his fear and timidity. He temporized and aggravated the LORD. Finally, "the spirit of the LORD departed from Saul."

Jesus used images of wine production to teach about the importance of a certain kind of loss called pruning. He taught that pruning is needed both in his kingdom generally and in our lives individually. He said, "I am the true vine, and my Father is the vinegrower. He removes every branch in me that bears no fruit. Every branch that bears fruit he prunes to make it bear more fruit. You have already been cleansed by the word that I have spoken to you. Abide in me as I abide in you. Just as the branch cannot bear fruit by itself unless it abides in the vine, neither can you unless you abide in me. I am the vine, you are the branches." Jesus loses entire branches in the parable, and the branches that remain are cut back to make them more fruitful. We are those branches. Loss is central to the teaching of Jesus.

Not all losses are bad. This is an opportunity for some pruning. "Do not say, 'Why were the former days better than these?' For it is not from wisdom that you ask this." Look for the opportunities in your losses.

twenty-five

Laughter

For everything there is a season, and a time for every matter under heaven: a time to weep, and a time to laugh. (Ecclesiastes 3:1, 4)

At the beginning of a jury trial, the jury is selected through a process called *voir dire*. The judge, the prosecution, and the defense ask a series of questions of the pool of potential jurors to determine whether they have any biases that could affect their judgment. There was a large jury pool for my trial – more than two hundred people. It was a tense process for me and my family. These people ultimately determine how the trial goes.

We had been going through jury selection a couple of hours when a woman raised her hand. She was a pleasant-looking woman in her midthirties. She told the judge that she thought she knew me and my family and that the more she looked at us the more convinced she was of it.

I was asked to sit a little off from the defense table so she could get a better look at me. The judge and my lawyers explored possible connections. Nothing. She lived in San Francisco, and I lived in Dallas. She said she may have known me through church, so we explored where she went to church and where I did.

During the conversation, I became very amused that two-hundred-plus people were sitting in a federal courthouse in San Francisco listening to a conversation about going to church. I involuntarily broke into a big grin.

The judge interrupted and said, "Ah, now Mr. Roberts is smiling. Maybe that will help you remember where you know him from."

It didn't, and this wonderful lady left the court after she told the judge, the prosecutors, and the assembled jury pool that there was no way she could vote to convict me.

The writer of Ecclesiastes while in a dour mood wrote, "Sorrow is better than laughter, for by sadness of countenance the heart is made glad." In a more even mood, he wrote that there was "a time to weep, and a time to laugh." It does not seem to have occurred to this fellow that weeping and laughing could occur at the same time.

After I was fired, I was very quickly advised that the "time to laugh" was right now. Laughter is a key element in resilience, or the ability to bounce back from a crisis. Beyond psychology, laughter stimulates certain hormones that help regulate perspective.

In the Book of Genesis, God comes to Abraham when Abraham is one hundred years old and reminds him of a promise made decades earlier that he would have a son with Sarah, his wife. She was then ninety years old and barren, and they had long since ceased having sexual relations. When God remade the promise, "Abraham fell on his face and laughed." God didn't react to this extraordinary response. Then the story gets really amusing. Three angels came and, within Sarah's hearing, told Abraham again that Sarah would have a son. Hearing this, "Sarah laughed to herself." God returned and, acting hurt, asked Abraham, "Why did Sarah laugh?...Is anything too wonderful for the LORD?" Sarah denied laughing. God scolded, "Oh yes, you did laugh."

There is no evidence God was actually upset. No disrespect was intended by Abraham or Sarah. The apparent disconnect between their reality and God's promise produced spontaneous laughter. God named the issue – was the promise "too wonderful?" Comedians say various disconnects from reality are the greatest source of humor. Every so often, my wife would say, "We are in 'Nah Nah' land." The disconnect in our lives could not have been greater.

From the beginning of my troubles, my wife and I made laughter an important part of our daily routine. We watched a broad range of comedians from Larry the Cable Guy and Jon Stewart to the Marx Brothers and Donald O'Connor (who sang "Make 'Em Laugh" in the movie *Singing in the Rain*). During one of the worst days of my trial, we went to see a movie by a British comedian and were able to summon up laughs in the midst of sheer terror. There is a scene in *How to Murder Your Wife* where Jack Lemmon turns that sheer terror into the finest physical comedy. We bought the DVD and replayed that part of the movie many times. The terror was still there, but we could step outside of it for a minute and laugh.

There is a famous recent painting of Jesus laughing out loud. Find a copy of it, and put it in your wallet. This is "a time to laugh" as often as you are able.

twenty-six

Prayer

Rejoice always, pray without ceasing, give thanks in all circumstances; for this is the will of God in Christ Jesus for you.
Do not quench the Spirit. (1 Thessalonians 5:16–19)

I was given a personal advantage when it comes to prayer. As soon as I could form sentences, my parents taught me to pray and prayed with me every night. Mom and Dad showed me how simple prayer is. The structure of prayer is flexible, and God is broadly tolerant of what and how things are said, as long as you take time to hear the response.

About twenty years ago, I studied the actual content of prayer. I concluded that there were basically only two prayers. The first, stripped to its essentials, goes like this: "Help, LORD." The second, in its essentials, is, "Thank you, God." The rest is elaboration.

A few years ago, the singer Carrie Underwood had a huge hit with a song about a driver caught up in a world of distractions who hits an unnoticed patch of black ice. As the car spins out of control, the driver throws up her hands and prays, "Jesus, take the wheel! Save me from this road I'm on." Here is a third prayer. The evangelicals call this giving your problem over to the LORD.

In Vasily Grossman's novel *Life and Fate*, the main character, a Soviet nuclear theorist at the time of the Battle of Stalingrad (1943), comes under suspicion and is placed on leave while the authorities decide what to do with him. Friends and family pull away. Alone, he begins to ponder the parallels to Stalin's Great Terror of 1937. He thinks, "How can one ever describe those nights and that extraordinary sense of both doom and innocence?"

After I was fired, I experienced "that extraordinary sense." What I remembered about events four to six years prior did not seem to warrant the gathering crisis. Not understanding what was taking place at my former employer, I made the common error of wondering if I was missing something. I began to question the quality and adequacy of my memory. I spent a lot of time curled up in bed trying to work through this.

A day or two into 2007, about two months before I was indicted, I was sitting alone at the kitchen table feeling very bad. I bowed my head and prayed, "God, I am stupid and afraid. I am relying completely on you. I am trusting you and want your will to be done." From that moment, the door was opened for me to trust God completely.

In the following months, I had almost weekly opportunities to thank God as reams of documents and testimony began to validate my memory and give it needed context. At trial there wasn't a single day where I could not see the hand of God at work and give thanks.

On Sundays during the trial, my wife and I went to church at Glide Memorial Methodist Church on the border of San Francisco's Tenderloin District. The church's theme song-prayer is a rock 'n' roll version of Fanny Crosby's classic hymn "Pass Me Not, O Gentle Savior." Glide's signature addition is a lengthy chant: "While on others you are calling, do not pass me by, do not pass me by...." This chorus came to me every day walking into court, at each break, and walking back out of the courthouse. There was no more natural or snappier way to pray, "Help, LORD."

Jesus was always in prayer. Mark tells a wonderfully simple story about this. "In the morning, while it was still very dark, he got up and went out to a deserted place, and there he prayed." Once you get started, a person under accusation will really have no trouble praying without ceasing.

So...pray. Do it in song, in words, or in groans. Do it out loud or silently. God already knows what you need and will give you the particulars of what to pray for.

twenty-seven

Prayer for Enemies

Bless those who persecute you; bless and do not curse them. Do not repay anyone evil for evil, but take thought for what is noble in the sight of all. Do not be overcome by evil, but overcome evil with good. (Romans 12:14, 17, 21)

When thrown into a dangerous pit for the first time, a person is likely to use muscles he or she never needed before to climb out. Kneeling down to pray, the accused will soon confront the teaching of Jesus about loving your enemies. In the Sermon on the Mount, Jesus said, "You have heard that it was said, 'You shall love your neighbor and hate your enemy.' But I say to you, Love your enemies and pray for those who persecute you."

For me, like most people, having enemies – real enemies – is itself a new experience. Previously, I had rivals maybe and competitors certainly, but having someone working hard and spending lots of money to put me into prison or otherwise destroy me was new. Loving this sort of person was hard to imagine.

Praying for my persecutors was likewise difficult. Certain prayers in the Psalms leapt to mind, such as, "Deliver me, O my God! For you strike all my enemies on the cheek; you break the teeth of the wicked," and "My times are in your hand; deliver me from the hand of my enemies and persecutors...Do not let me be put to shame, O LORD, for I call on you; let the wicked be put to shame; let them go dumbfounded to

Sheol [hell]." I have prayed these, in a strictly metaphorical sense, but I am certain that this is not what Jesus is talking about.

The apostle Paul suggests, "No, 'if your enemies are hungry, feed them; if they are thirsty, give them something to drink; for by doing this you will heap burning coals on their heads.'" The behavioral advice seems in line with the teaching of Jesus, but the motivation may be off.

I found it pretty natural to pray that my enemies would relax, stay flexible in their thinking and attitudes, and be enlightened as to the true facts. I realized I was praying for myself, not for my enemies.

There is a modern tendency to explain this teaching of Jesus in terms of the bad effect anger has emotionally. You need to release yourself from your anger, it is said, because the anger makes a bad situation worse *for you*. I do not doubt that, but Jesus gave a different reason for loving your enemies.

Jesus said we are to do this "so that you may be children of your Father in heaven; for he makes his sun rise on the evil and on the good, and sends rain on the righteous and on the unrighteous." In other words, Jesus is calling us to emulate God. This requires a switch in perspective.

"Enemy" is not a permanent status. Scripture reminds us that friends can become enemies, as with Judas and Jesus, and enemies can become friends, as with Herod and Pilate. The word "enemy" itself underscores the transient nature of being an enemy. It is formed from "in," meaning "not," as in "inadequate," and "amity," meaning "friendship." Literally, it just means "not a friend."

Considering the issue of enemies from the viewpoint of God, we learn that "whoever wishes to be a friend of the world becomes an enemy of God." Paul said, "[M]any live as enemies of the cross of Christ; ...their minds are set on earthly things." That makes each of us God's enemy at some point.

What is God's response to his enemies – us? "For while we were still weak, at the right time Christ died for the ungodly...For if while we were enemies, we were reconciled to God through the death of his Son, much more surely, having been reconciled, will we be saved by his life." God's response to his enemies is to offer reconciliation.

After I was indicted, I prayed for my enemies every day. It was not easy. For some I could get no further than, "God, I am praying for this fellow because you asked me to." For most I prayed that they would be richly blessed and have the courage to do what was right as they saw it. Over time I was fortified by two thoughts. The first was a Hindu proverb that "an angry man" and "a frightened man" will "never do the right thing." The LORD could reduce their anger and fear. The second was that these persons may not be able to pray for themselves. Since they had my attention, I may have been the right person to intercede for them.

While you are praying, pray for your enemies. It is one of those things you do without fully understanding. My prayers were hardly perfect, but praying for my enemies did not hurt me - or them. Only God knows where things will stand in these relationships when your troubles are finally over.

twenty-eight

Prayer for Others

An interesting thing happened when the actual date for my trial was scheduled. The date had, as expected, been moved twice, but I knew that September 16 was the real trial date. I quickly noticed that I was unable or unwilling to make plans for any event after September 16. As the emotionally dislocated protagonist in Murakami's *The Wind-Up Bird Chronicle* explained, "I had no plans, I said. Plans were simply something I did not have." I was missing the most important information about the time after that date – whether I would have any control over my schedule – and, therefore, my calendar was literally blank. My usable future ended on September 16.

As the date approached, my sense of isolation deepened. Nine days before the trial, communion was served at my church. I was kneeling at the rail waiting for the bread and grape juice when the senior pastor came up to me and patted me on the shoulder.

He said, "I've been praying for you."

I looked up to make sure it was him. We had never even discussed my situation. I smiled.

He asked, "Are you going to be OK?"

I answered cheerfully, "I think so." I bowed my head and thanked God for the senior pastor's prayers and this marvelous church.

That same day, my immediate family – about thirty-two people – were fasting and praying about the upcoming trial. I had never heard of them doing such a thing before.

That Sunday, these prayers pulled me out of my oddly suspended perspective and put me back into normal time.

I was deeply benefitted by the prayers of others. Word came to me very early (in that guarded way lawyers talk to each other) that "more people than you know are pulling for you." My wife never stopped praying. A close family friend prayed for me and with me frequently. He and my wife independently put me on one of the nation's largest prayer lists.

I didn't ask for any of this – the whole thing was so embarrassing – but they prayed for me anyway. Going into trial I thought, *How great a God is this who inspires us to pray for those who are in trouble?*

Epaphras of Colossae was a mighty prayer on behalf of his countrymen. He was one of Paul's colleagues in prison. Paul told the Colossians that Epaphras was "always wrestling in his prayers on your behalf." He seems to have deepened even Paul's understanding of intercessory prayer, or prayer on behalf of others. Paul told the Philippians about the unanticipated benefit his imprisonment was having for the spread of the gospel. He then noted, "I will continue to rejoice, for I know that through your prayers and the help of the Spirit of Jesus Christ this will turn out for my deliverance."

You can never tell how things will work out. Paul's deliverance wasn't the one he expected. Still, the prayers of the church sustained him and, as he hoped, he was able to preach the gospel in Rome.

In retrospect, I wish I would have been bolder in asking for the prayers of others. They were such a blessing to me. Now, I pray nightly for those in trouble, by name when I know them. It is a privilege to ask God's help for them.

It is not too early for you, the accused, to reach out to God on behalf of others. Others, including those you don't even know, are praying for you.

twenty-nine

Slowing Down

Now the boy Samuel was ministering to the LORD under Eli. The word of the
LORD was rare in those days; visions were not widespread... Samuel was
lying down in the temple of the LORD, where the ark of God was. Then the
LORD called, "Samuel! Samuel!" and he said, "Here I am!" and ran to Eli, and
said, "Here I am, for you called me." But he said, "I did not call; lie down
again." So he went and lay down... The LORD called Samuel again... And he
got up and went to Eli, and said, "Here I am, for you called me." Then Eli
perceived that the LORD was calling the boy. Therefore Eli said to Samuel,
"Go, lie down; and if he calls you, you shall say, 'Speak, LORD, for your servant is listening.'" So Samuel went and lay down in his place. Now the LORD
came and stood there, calling as before, "Samuel! Samuel!" And Samuel
said, "Speak, for your servant is listening." (1 Samuel 3: 1, 3–5, 8–10)

Someone asked me how I prepared myself for my criminal trial. I said I
prayed, I laughed, and I slowed down.

Before I was fired, I was constantly on the move with meetings,
electronic communications, and travel. The travel was so bad that my
New Year's resolution for 2006 was to spend three full weeks each
month in Texas. No one believed it was possible. When I was fired, it
was like going from sixty miles an hour to a hard stop.

Afterward, I was reminded in the letter of James about the benefits
to "the rich in being brought low." He said, "[T]he rich will disappear
like a flower in the field. For the sun rises with its scorching heat and

withers the field; its flower falls, and its beauty perishes. It is the same way with the rich; in the midst of a busy life, they will wither away."

There is a physical slowing down, and there is a mental slowing down. Many of the choices in everyday life are a single choice presented repeatedly. We buy a certain kind of milk and bread, wear a certain type of pants, listen to a certain type of music, agree to this language in a particular kind of contract, hire a person with a certain level of experience, and so on. Much of our personal efficiency comes from performing these simple repetitive tasks without extraordinary amounts of thought.

Once accused, I was presented with choices not faced before. There is no advantage to the accused in acting quickly. In fact, I noticed that it was the government and my accusers who were trying to speed me up and up the ante on me. Even if I knew what I was going to do, I would sleep on all major decisions just to watch what thoughts presented themselves after I settled on a proposed course of action.

Laughter, prayer, and slowing down became a personal program to be aware of God's hand in my life. The stories of the Bible show how important it is to God that we slow down. When the LORD came to them, Moses was quietly tending a flock of sheep far from anybody, the boy prophet Samuel was "lying down in the temple of the LORD" and John was "in the spirit on the LORD's day" in exile on the island of Patmos. Jesus was always retiring to the mountains, gardens, and wildernesses to be with God.

There is much written about making space for God. Most of it deals with how to find time in a busy life to pray and meditate. By and large, busyness is not the main problem of the accused. I have an excellent coffee shop near my house. Now they know me by name. I went there at least five days a week to look things over, think about suggestions for my lawyers, and count my blessings. Every night, I went on a long walk with my dog. One evening, I was particularly upset. I finally looked up at the moon, which that night was full and huge. It reminded me that God was with me.

There is more to slowing down than thinking. The point of slowing down is to listen. An active mind can quickly be filled with anxiety.

Prayer, meditation, and fasting quiet the mind and discipline the mind to trust in the LORD.

On that LORD's day on Patmos, Jesus told John, "Listen! I am standing at the door, knocking; if you hear my voice and open the door, I will come in to you and eat with you, and you with me."

Slow down. Listen.

thirty

Strength

Laurence Gonzales observes that once people accept that they are in a survival situation, they make a choice. "Some give up and die. Others stop denying and begin surviving." At that point, fortunately, "You don't have to be an elite performer. You don't have to be perfect. You just have to get on with it and do the next right thing."

What is needed is the strength "to get on with it." The Bible has quite a lot to say about strength. Isaiah affirms: "The Lord is the everlasting God, the Creator of the ends of the earth. He does not faint or grow weary; his understanding is unsearchable. He gives power to the faint, and strengthens the powerless. Even youths will faint and be weary, and the young will fall exhausted; but those who wait for the Lord shall renew their strength, they shall mount up with wings like eagles, they shall run and not be weary, they shall walk and not faint."

I was frankly surprised as I went about "getting on with it and doing the next right thing" at the amount of physical, mental, and spiritual strength that was available to me. I found enormous personal resources that I did not think I had.

From time to time, I stopped to consider this uncanny strength, and I could see the hand of God laying up reserves throughout my life that I would use later. The following is personal to me but may help point you to your own sources of strength.

I had no trouble getting around in the Bible and the Jewish and Christian tradition because my parents, when I was a child, and my wife, when I was an adult, insisted that I go to church and pray and practice the other spiritual disciplines.

The prosecutors did much finger wagging about my law degree, but it was very useful in understanding what was going on in the evidence and with the court. Also, one of my law professors told us that every criminal defendant has the right to force the government to prove the case against him. That simple insight came back twenty-five years later with potent force.

From my mother, I think, I got a somewhat contrarian spirit. Throughout my life, I could always see the other side. I always thought that if I were a judge, I would be the fellow dissenting or disagreeing with the majority. This trait can be uncomfortable in normal settings, but it is a godsend when you are actually standing in opposition to your government.

From a former boss of mine – who is not a lawyer – I got a clear understanding of the importance of persistence in litigation. In a heated conversation with me when I was working for him, he insisted that winning a lawsuit was "all about will." Then, over the next ten years, he showed me what his words meant through the example of his own life.

Many years before I was indicted, a family friend had invited my wife and me to go with him to minister to prisoners. He took me from the yard to the pod where the prisoners lived and slept and then to the solitary-confinement cells. He introduced me to former prisoners moving forward with their lives. These experiences helped me thoughtfully consider the alternatives available to me. Once my legal troubles began, this family friend became the most important of the guides God sent. He had been through this experience before.

Fear is considered good in a survival situation because it motivates you to focus and keep going. Panic, on the other hand, is to be avoided because it leads you to stupid actions that destroy your strength. In Isaiah, God says, "See, I am laying in Zion a foundation stone, a tested stone, a sure foundation: 'One who trusts will not panic.'" It is clear from the statement that the trust that keeps you from panic is trust in the LORD. The Psalmist says very simply, "My flesh and my heart may fail, but God is the strength of my heart and my portion forever."

Like me, the accused will relate to the Psalmist's image of "an army encamp[ed]" and "war ris[ing] up" against you. It is true that God is the stronghold of your life.

God has, and will, make sufficient resources available to you in this situation. Call on them, and call on God. Look for where God has strengthened you.

thirty-one
Support

Do not fear, for I am with you, do not be afraid, for I am
your God; I will strengthen you, I will help you, I will uphold
you with my victorious right hand. (Isaiah 41·10)

The week I was indicted I received two pieces of paper from my government. The first was entitled "The United States of America against Kent H. Roberts." The second was entitled "The United States Securities and Exchange Commission against Kent H. Roberts." There was no ambiguity about who they intended to imprison and impoverish. It was the government against *me*. I needed help!

During the exodus from Egypt to the Promised Land, the Israelites were attacked by a group led by a man named Amalek. Moses asked Joshua to fight the Amalekites while Moses stood on a nearby hill holding up the staff of God for the Israelites to see. "Whenever Moses held up his hand, Israel prevailed; and whenever he lowered his hand, Amalek prevailed." Even a young man would quickly tire when holding his arms aloft. Moses was over eighty years old. "Moses' hands grew weary." Moses could not, by himself, relieve the natural fatigue of his arms. Moses's brother Aaron and a man named Hur stepped forward in the crisis. "Aaron and Hur held up his hands, one on one side, and the other on the other side; so his hands were steady until the sun set. And Joshua defeated Amalek and his people with the sword."

My Hur was my dedicated team of lawyers, and my Aaron was my heroic wife.

In the spring of 2008, the level of concern in our house about the coming trial rose perceptibly. Previously, we had told our daughter that I had been fired, it was a big scandal, and the government was suing me. We hadn't told her a lot more. One afternoon that spring, she asked me if the government was still suing me. I said yes. She asked if they were trying to put me in jail. I said yes. There was a long pause. She finally asked, "Do you have a lawyer?" I said yes. There was a much longer pause, and I told her I had some very good lawyers helping me and I was a lawyer and could help them with the case. My daughter visibly relaxed.

Like Hur, my lawyers took on my case without reservation, poured their hearts into it, and looked out only for my best interests. If you have that, you are blessed. I have a friend who did not have that, so he fired his first lawyer, hired a good lawyer, and did very well.

Very early in this crisis, I started taking stock of which losses I thought I would be able to bear. The one loss I doubted I could bear was the loss of my wife. Many marriages do not survive a criminal indictment. For almost three years, it was like we were stranded on a desert island with no one else to talk to and nothing else to talk about. The toll on my wife was tremendous. She developed a life-threatening condition in response to the crisis. Too many times, I was awakened early in the morning by her quiet sobs. Almost nobody signs up for this kind of stress. I would have understood if she had done what other wives often do. No one deserves this much pain, least of all her. Ultimately, the decision whether to stay was hers.

Like Aaron, she not only stayed with me; she strongly supported me and never left my side for a moment. That was God's richest blessing.

If your spouse stays with you, thank God. While you are at it, forgive every imperfection because your spouse is forgiving a lot more than you ever will. If your spouse leaves, thank him or her for all the time you two had together.

Trust in God and, as promised in the Book of Isaiah, God will find ways to strengthen you, help you, and uphold you.

thirty-two

Endurance

But the one who endures to the end will be saved. (Matthew 10:22)

During the summer before my trial, I heard a song on the radio that had the refrain, "If you are goin' through hell, keep on going." I turned the radio up very loud to listen to that statement again (and again).

"Going through hell." This was a song for me! Being accused of a crime is one of life's most alarming experiences. I remember looking at those charts where they rate on a scale of one hundred the stress that various events bring into a person's life. I wanted to see where being indicted ranked against divorce, illness, job loss, the death of a child, and so on. It wasn't even on the chart! With more than seven million persons caught in the US criminal justice system, it can't have been an unknown experience. The list makers must not have deemed the stress of the accused worthy to be measured.

People don't use metaphors to describe this experience; they use this experience as a metaphor to describe other bad experiences. Poor Dad. He's going through a time of trial. Poor Grandmother. She's a great spirit imprisoned in her failing body.

It took me a second to understand the second part of the refrain. "If you are goin' through hell, keep on going." Oh, I get it. Don't stop. Don't get stuck. Get out of hell before the devil knows you are there.

Some days, life is a matter of brute persistence and endurance. Jesus said, "But the one who endures to the end will be saved." The writer of

Hebrews referred to the example of Jesus enduring the cross and to the martyrs who "suffered mocking and flogging, and even chains and imprisonment...[T]hey went about...destitute, persecuted, tormented – of whom the world was not worthy...Therefore," the writer of Hebrews concluded, "let us run with perseverance the race that is set before us."

The Apostles' Creed is an ancient affirmation of the Christian faith that is still recited in churches today. It reminds us that after Jesus died, "he descended into hell." This is a reminder of the teaching of the apostle Peter that Jesus "went and made proclamation to the spirits in prison." I started adding some emphasis to that part of my daily declaration of faith.

The scriptures are clear that God is with us in our earthly hells. The ancient Hebrews used the word "Sheol" for what we think of as hell. The Psalmist affirmed, "Where can I go from your spirit? Or where can I flee from your presence? If I ascend to heaven, you are there; if I make my bed in Sheol, you are there." King David's most famous psalm, "The Lord is my shepherd," contains a very pertinent assurance: "Yea, though I walk through the valley of the shadow of death, I will fear no evil; for thou art with me; thy rod and thy staff they comfort me."

Endurance is hard. Perseverance is difficult. There are very few people cheering you on in this particular race. To the contrary, you are broadly vilified. The government may even offer you an "easy way out" of the pain. It may come in the form of a plea deal. A plea deal may make perfect sense for you. For me, it was a false promise made to further the prosecutors' goals. In the Book of Revelation, John is shown "the lake that burns with fire and sulfur, which is the second death." In it are mostly the persons you might expect – "the faithless, the polluted, the murderers, the fornicators, the sorcerers, the idolaters, and all liars." What was interesting to me, when I read it again during my time of trouble, was that the very first on the list were "the cowardly." As John frequently reminded, "Here is a call for the endurance and faith of the saints."

As previously indicated, on weekends during my trial, we went to worship at Glide Memorial Methodist Church. During the opening call to worship, they ran a slide show. One of the slides said, "When you are going through hell, keep going."

As you are going through hell, God is with you. God has been through there before. God knows the way out. God will lead you. "The one who endures to the end will be saved."

thirty-three
Joy

This is the day that the Lᴏʀᴅ has made; let us rejoice
and be glad in it. (Psalm 118:24)

Finally, the day for human judgment will come. For me, it was Friday, October 3, 2008, the third day of jury deliberations. About lunchtime the court clerk called and told us that the jury had sent out a note. The note said that they had reached a unanimous conclusion on two questions and were deadlocked on the remaining question. The judge asked the jury to fill out the verdict form as far as they could. Back in the jury room, the jury did and then came out and handed the envelope with the partially completed verdict form to the judge. She looked at it and started asking the jury whether they were actually deadlocked and whether coming back on Monday would make any difference. They said that additional deliberation would not make a difference.

The judge ordered me to stand up to receive the verdict. I secretly braced myself against a nearby table. The judge told me that the jury found me not guilty on count one and not guilty on count two and declared a mistrial on count three. Silence. And then I could hear my wife behind me in the courtroom crying. While the jury was still there, I asked if I could go to my wife. I mouthed "thank you" to the jury and then went back to her and held her while she cried. Several of the jurors were weeping with her. The jury was excused. Then the judge turned to the government and said, "I would strongly recommend against pursuing this any further." The prosecutor said she would have the paperwork dropping the rest of the case finalized the next business day.

And so it was. Aside from the day I got married and the days my children were born, sitting with my wife in that courtroom on October 3 is the greatest moment of my life. The joy is just as vivid now. I still tear up when I remember it. We celebrate it every year.

After being exploited in Egypt as slaves for four hundred years, the children of Israel were permitted to leave. Then Pharaoh reneged and sent the army to bring them back to slavery. The LORD made a way for the Israelites to escape through the Red Sea. When the army tried to follow, it was drowned. On the other side, "the prophet Miriam, Aaron's [and Moses's] sister, took a tambourine in her hand; and all the women went out after her with tambourines and with dancing. And Miriam sang to them: 'Sing to the LORD, for he has triumphed gloriously; horse and rider he has thrown into the sea.'" The descendants of the Israelites have celebrated their freedom every year since!

After 250 years of slavery, African Americans were freed. Though their practical status was uncertain and varied from region to region for the next one hundred years, the descendants of those slaves have celebrated their freedom every year since. Like the ancient Hebrews who inspired them, they sing, "Lift every voice and sing, till earth and heaven ring; ring with the harmonies of liberty; let our rejoicing rise high as the listening skies, let it resound as loud as the rolling sea." And the harmonies continue. My acquittal meant I was free to vote one month later in the election that resulted in our first African American president.

I am aware that not everyone who reads this will be acquitted. I do not think God loves me more or that I did something better. But God does love me, and I would be lying if I denied my joy. In fact, it is my duty to proclaim it. "He put a new song in my mouth, a song of praise to our God. Many will see and fear, and put their trust in the LORD."

Someday, one way or the other, you will be free. If you trust wholly in the LORD, you may already be free. Alexander Solzhenitsyn exclaimed from the vast Soviet gulag, "My name? I am the Interstellar Wanderer! They have tightly bound my body, but my soul is beyond their power." Thomas á Kempis taught, "LORD, one who desires perfection must make it his first task to keep his mind at all times set on heavenly things. By so doing, he can pass carefree through many troubles, not as one who has not the wit to realize the dangers that beset him, but in the strength of a free mind, unfettered by undue attachments to worldly things."

Trust in the LORD. Move forward "in the strength of a free mind."

thirty-four
Withdrawal

In the morning, while it was still very dark, [Jesus] got up and
went out to a deserted place, and there he prayed. And Simon
and his companions hunted for him. (Mark 1:35-36)

The day I was acquitted, my lawyers organized a celebration. The party was loud and fun. I was the quietest person there. I was so closed in emotionally that all I could think about was how tired I was.

A few days later, I joked that once the still-pending Securities and Exchange Commission case against me was over, I was going to take a vow of silence. I love to talk and write, so that was saying something. Six months later, when the SEC voluntarily dropped the case, I was invited to speak at a national conference – the same one I had been scheduled to address three years earlier during the week I was fired. I declined the invitation, saying, "I would rather never speak again than speak before I am ready."

A couple of years later, I reread a story that had comforted me when the government was after me. It was about a man named Narcissus (no relation to the mythic character that Sigmund Freud wrote about) who was the bishop of the Christian church in Jerusalem during the second and third centuries. The historian Eusebius preserved this story about him:

His energy and conscientiousness were more than some insignificant nonentities could bear. Knowing themselves guilty of a long series of misdemeanors, they were afraid that

121

conviction and punishment awaited them. To avoid this, they devised an intrigue against him and besmirched him with a horrid slander. Then, to convince their hearers, they bolstered up their accusations with oaths. One swore: "If it isn't true, may I be burnt to death!" Another: "May my body be wasted by a foul disease!" A third: "May I lose my sight!" But no amount of swearing made any of the faithful take any notice, for no one could fail to see the unshakable integrity and blameless character of Narcissus.

But he himself was greatly distressed by their dastardly allegations, and in addition he had long ago embraced the philosophic life; so, turning his back on the church community, he fled into a remote and desert area, where he remained in hiding for many years.

However, the great eye of Justice did not remain unmoved by these events, but very soon brought upon those perjured scoundrels the curses with which they had bound themselves. The first saw the house which he occupied ablaze from top to bottom for no other cause whatever than a tiny spark that settled on the roof in the night, and he and all his family were burnt to ashes; the second felt his entire body from head to toe permeated by the very disease he had named as his penalty; the third, seeing the fate of the others and dreading the inescapable judgment of all-seeing God, publicly confessed his share in the intrigue, but in his remorse he wore himself out with so many lamentations, and poured out such a flood of tears, that he lost the sight of both eyes. Such was the price these men paid for their lies...

In his time Narcissus appeared from nowhere, as if restored to life, and was invited by the brethren to resume his prelateship, for he was admired by all even more than before because of his withdrawal and philosophic life – above all because of the judgment by which God had vindicated him.

Before my trial and until the SEC voluntarily dropped its case, I focused on God's judgment of the three false witnesses. As Paul reminded the Romans, "[L]eave room for the wrath of God; for it is written, 'Vengeance is mine, I will repay, says the LORD.'"

When I looked at the story fresh, I was struck by the fact that even though Narcissus was vindicated, "he fled into a remote and desert place, where he remained in hiding for many years."

I realized that I had withdrawn as well. Actually, I had never reemerged after the resolution of the accusations. A friend of mine said it well: "It's not like you can flip a switch and everything's back to normal." After years of having my words twisted, I self-censor every thought and statement. I ask, "How could this be misconstrued?" Even now, a part of me argues against my being so open in this Meditation. I also have lingering fears. I feel like a dog that has been kicked. The most mundane conflict can stir up strong apprehension.

There are deeper issues that have to be resolved. The question *What do I do with this experience?* has to be answered. Inability to answer this question is paralyzing. Answering it incorrectly can be just as devastating – in the long run. At the deepest level, withdrawal is necessary to have time to address the most basic questions: *Can others be trusted? Can I be trusted? Can God be trusted?*

In retreating, Bishop Narcissus followed a long tradition documented in the Bible. The most interesting example is the opening chapter of Mark, which contains three separate instances of Jesus withdrawing. The first was when "the Spirit immediately drove him out into the wilderness [for] forty days" (verses 12 – 13). Another was when Jesus "stayed out in the country" because he had become too famous to go into town openly (verses 43 – 45). My favorite of the three is where Mark tells how, after an evening of casting out demons, "[i]n the morning, while it was still dark, [Jesus] got up and went out to a deserted place, and there he prayed. And Simon and his companions hunted for him" (verses 35 – 36).

It is natural and holy to withdraw. God wants us to understand what this experience means and what should happen next. This is the good news: Jesus was just beginning his work. In this, as in other stories in the Bible, withdrawal marks the beginning – not the end. Through prayer, mediation, and communion, the LORD redirects us. Then, like Bishop Narcissus, we can "appear from nowhere, as if restored to life."

thirty-five

Forgiving

For if you forgive others their trespasses, your heavenly Father
will also forgive you; but if you do not forgive others, neither will
your Father forgive your trespasses. (Matthew 6:14–15)

A few years after the accusation against me was resolved, I attended a week-long conference on reconciliation and restorative justice. The topic of forgiveness was raised the first day, and we were each asked to identify a time when it was hard for us to forgive.

An older woman in the group told us that she and her daughter had been attacked many years earlier. Her daughter had been murdered. She herself had been left for dead. She attended the trial of the attacker and had visited him in prison. Then her voice broke. She said she had prayed and prayed, but she couldn't forgive him. Then she said, "And I know if I don't forgive him, God won't forgive me. So I'm stuck."

I wanted to comfort her and say, *No! You are wrong. A loving God would understand. God will forgive you your inability to forgive.* But I held back. No one else said anything to correct her.

She was right. In the Sermon on the Mount, Jesus said, "[I]f you do not forgive others, neither will your Father forgive your trespasses."

Jesus was once asked, "[H]ow often should I forgive? As often as seven times?"

Jesus replied, "Not seven times, but, I tell you, seventy-seven times."

Not satisfied that his hearers understood the importance of his teaching, Jesus then told them a parable about a king. A man owed the king a massive debt. The man pleaded for more time to pay. The king went further and completely forgave the debt. The forgiven man then threw a person who owed him a small debt into debtors' prison, ignoring that person's pleas for mercy. The king found out and had the first man "tortured until he would pay his entire debt." Then Jesus said, "So my heavenly Father will also do to every one of you if you do not forgive your brother or sister from your heart."

In earlier drafts of these Meditations, I did not deal with forgiveness. I asked a pastor to read a draft. He correctly called me out on the omission. I hadn't left it out because I didn't see the issue. I left it out because I wasn't ready to come clean about forgiveness.

Every night, when I recite the Lord's Prayer, I place a mental reservation at the part that says, "And forgive us our debts, as we forgive our debtors."

There are a few persons I have not forgiven.

The resolution of an accusation often happens in an established process, whether in the criminal justice system or elsewhere. Most of the people involved are just playing a role. A man named James Woodward was convicted in 1981 and served twenty-seven years in prison for a crime he did not commit. He gave a lot of thought to the people operating the process that unjustly imprisoned him. He said, "I figured out a long time ago that my being sent to prison wasn't anything personal. It was just two guys – the prosecutors – looking at their career, trying to do a job. And the jury – they only went along with what the prosecutor said. So I had to get those kinds of thoughts, or any kinds of malevolent thoughts, out of my mind. That's what destroys a man in prison. You know, just constantly being frustrated and angry by things he can't change."

Of my specific accusers, I found some easy enough to forgive. A couple of fellows were eagerly zealous in pressing the case against me. This blinded them to the fact that they were actually helping me in important ways. They have the clownish charm of really angry children for me now.

There are a small handful of men, however, with whom I still have a problem. These are men I trusted, but who, in my view, pursued their own interests at my expense. These are the enemies I was praying for before my trial. Now I know that it is much easier to pray for your enemies than to forgive them.

I am not letting myself off the hook. These men do not threaten me now. I live a thousand miles or more from each of them. I do not run in their circles anymore. Forgiving them would not involve any change in my external behavior. I wouldn't even have to tell them. They would probably laugh at the thought that they needed to be forgiven.

All that is involved is one little switch in my thinking. And I am *not willing* to make it!

Clearly, I will lose something very important to me if I forgive these men. It is very important, but I can't even tell myself what it is. God wants me to lose it, but I want to keep it. Whatever it is is so important to me that I literally defy the God who delivered me from these accusers. I must be crazy.

I think there are situations where forgiveness is more than putting away the feelings and seeing the other person's side of the story.

I keep considering one of my accusers in the light of Jesus's teaching about forgiveness. My trust and admiration for him before my troubles was very high. Just before I was fired, he invited me to his son's *bris* circumcision ceremony and re-extended the invitation the weekend that I was fired.

As his role became clearer, I gave away my large collection of bowties, the fashion preference we shared. When we deposed him, he wanted to pull me aside to share his joy that his daughter had been accepted to Stanford. At trial he snuck up behind me and surprised me by shaking my hand after he testified against me. He told me he missed me. When my verdict was being read, he was across the town threatening me – through my lawyers – that after I was convicted, my former employer, which he represented, was going to take my home and cars (a nine-year-old Honda Odyssey and a fourteen-year-old Ford Explorer) and leave my family homeless.

After the government case was over, I told a mutual friend about this behavior and he said, "[This person] is dead to me!"

Yet he is not dead to me. Why isn't he one of the accusers that I just forgive and leave in the past? I would never hire him again. I would never take his advice again. But when the government gave me back my passport and I could travel abroad again, I found that I would think of him whenever I visited a historic European or Middle Eastern synagogue. Before my time of troubles, I would have told him about it or sent a souvenir.

Forgiveness is sometimes very hard.

thirty-six

Healing

Seven months after I was indicted, I considered my situation. I thought, *Sometimes I feel like some large chunk of me has been killed.* I could still function, but I reflected on the story of a world-famous woman who had been in a horrible car wreck that wrapped parts of the car tightly around her body. She remained alive and conscious for several hours, but when they removed her from the car, she quickly bled to death. The twisted metal of the car had been the only thing holding her together.

Am I like her? I wondered. *Is the pressure of this situation the only thing holding me together? What about when the crisis is over? What are my wounds, and how bad are they?*

Frequently, soldiers who have performed heroically in the heat of battle find, after the conflict is resolved, that they have suffered injuries that were concealed by adrenaline and the urgency of the mission. When the accusation is resolved – for better or worse, justly or unjustly – inspect yourself for wounds. I assure you they will be there.

My wounds took a while to become obvious. Right after the SEC voluntarily dismissed its case against me, I sat down with a friend to begin networking to find a job. He asked me to describe my perfect job. Over the next five minutes, I passionately described working with the legal team I had assembled at my former employer and the tremendous help we had given the company. I was interested by my level of enthusiasm. At the time, I felt satisfaction rather than pain in the recollection.

Later, I began to reconnect with members of my old team. They confirmed rumors I had heard about the abuse the team had suffered in the panic that followed my firing. This information engaged my protective instincts and made me realize how profoundly I felt the loss of the team. The hurt was compounded by years of unrelenting rejection letters in my job search. These letters helped me understand that, most likely, there was no possibility for me to build another team like it.

The letter to the Hebrews was written following harsh persecution of the young Christian church. The writer asked his readers to "recall those earlier days when, after you had been enlightened, you endured a hard struggle with sufferings, sometimes being publicly exposed to abuse and persecution, and sometimes being partners with those so treated." The writer counseled endurance and then turned the discussion to the open wounds.

"Endure trials for the sake of discipline," he wrote. "Now, discipline always seems painful rather than pleasant at the time."

The writer of Hebrews takes for granted that spiritual healing – "the peaceful fruit of righteousness" – will occur. After all, "[t]he LORD is my shepherd, I shall not want...he restores my soul."

The writer of Hebrews warns against actions that thwart the recovery, saying, "[M]ake straight paths for your feet, so that what is lame will not be put out of joint." A bad course of treatment can compound an injury. As you consider your personal open wound, be careful. The Bible makes clear the right way to act. If your case turned out OK, don't think you can start skipping your prayers. If your case went badly, don't give up hope. Jesus promises, "Nothing is covered up that will not be uncovered, and nothing secret that will not become known." If the accusation was correct and you are burdened with guilt, God has provided a "straight path" for repentance and forgiveness. In any event, don't lie to yourself or make excuses. Don't give into bitterness, cynicism, fear, or despair. "[The LORD] heals the brokenhearted, and binds up their wounds."

My wound is not about my team. Each of them is doing well as best as I can tell. My wound is, at the deepest level, about my fear of being useless. It rises up in me every week or so. In my rational mind, I quickly see my error. I ask myself, *Useless to whom?*

I struggle with the question, *Will I contribute again?* If this is a remnant of personal ambition, I know it is a false path for me. The real question is, *Will I be useful to God? What will that look like?*

The LORD reminded the prophet Jeremiah, "Blessed are those who trust in the LORD, whose trust is the LORD. They shall be like a tree planted by water, sending out its roots by the stream. It shall not fear when the heat comes, and its leaves shall stay green; in the year of drought it is not anxious, and it does not cease to bear fruit."

Is it too late for me? Moses, stuck in the desert tending his father-in-law's sheep, was eighty years old when the LORD called him back to Egypt to lead his people out of slavery.

That is the answer I give myself. It is never too late to be useful to God.

thirty-seven
Consolation

Blessed be the God and Father of our Lord Jesus Christ, the Father of mercies and the God of all consolation, who consoles us in all our affliction, so that we may be able to console those who are in any affliction with the consolation with which we ourselves are consoled by God. (2 Corinthians 1:3–4)

If my time of troubles has any greater meaning, it is the meaning the apostle Paul stresses in the opening of his second letter to the church at Corinth. By the time he wrote the letter, Paul had frequently been on the receiving end of community justice in the form of "beatings, imprisonments, [and] riots." In the letter, he listed his "imprisonments, with countless floggings, and often near death. Five times I have received from the Jews the forty lashes minus one. Three times I have been beaten with rods. Once I received a stoning."

In the face of this experience, Paul opens the letter with a great affirmation: "Blessed be the God and Father of our Lord Jesus Christ, the Father of mercies and the God of all consolation, who consoles us in all our affliction, so that we may be able to console those who are in any affliction with the consolation with which we ourselves are consoled by God."

To "console" is to alleviate the grief, sense of loss, or trouble of another. The word has the same root as "solace" and is sometimes translated as "comfort," though our modern notions of comfort tend to obscure the deeply soul-healing sense of assuagement of grief, loss, and trouble that "consolation" still conveys.

Each phrase of Paul's affirmation resonates for me as one who was accused.

"Blessed be the God and Father of our LORD Jesus Christ, the Father of mercies." God made clear that the LORD was present throughout my time of troubles. The life of Jesus provided continuous examples of how to conduct myself in unfamiliar and treacherous times.

"The God of all consolation." Consolation was freely available to me. It came in many forms. It was delivered personally, through others I knew or came to know, through the scriptures, the lives of faithful Christians, and the keen understanding of the great novelists.

"Who consoles us in all our affliction." The first message is that God consoles us. The second message is that God consoles us "in all our affliction." Society, including sometimes the church, spends a lot of energy sorting worthy from unworthy affliction and worthy from unworthy sufferers. God doesn't make the same distinction.

"So that." God has something God wants in this situation. What is God's purpose?

"We may be able to console those who are in any affliction with the consolation with which we ourselves are consoled by God." This is our task. We are to "console those who are in any affliction."

The accused has been given a special insight. Society will never look or sound the same. One cannot be accused of a crime and watch the television or read the newspaper the same way again. We have sojourned in the criminal justice system. We have experienced the pain of the accused and at least contemplated the anger and despair of the prisoner personally. We know how naïve the popular slogan "the system works" really is.

I feel like I have been prepared through this experience to help others who have been accused. Henri Nouwen described the "Wounded Healer," a person whose specific pain becomes a bridge for the redemption of others. He wrote, "The great illusion of leadership is to think that man can be led out of the desert by someone who has never been there."

Within days of my being fired, my father-in-law flew out from Los Angeles to encourage me by telling me about a time he had been accused of wrongdoing and stood his ground. My distress was such that I don't remember a word he said, but I remember tremendous comfort afterward. A family friend called me to share his experience of being tried for embezzlement. He told me the situation I was in would be worth it if even one person came to Christ because of my experience. One of my city's most prominent attorneys and his wife, whom I used to work with, took me and my wife out to dinner and told us about the months he spent under threat of federal indictment. He reassured us we would come through it, however it turned out. I could not have heard these messages from anyone else.

A few months later, a fellow executive was publicly fired by my former employer. The press release gave a certain impression about the reasons. I was still under a cloud. I couldn't get him on the phone that day, but I asked his son to tell him, "I know exactly how you feel. You and your family are in our prayers." In the coming years, he and I shared encouragement and our faith as we each worked toward vindication. The opportunities to share the consolation I received continue.

So this is what I say to you: God will not pass you by. God is with you. Those whom God has consoled are with you. Someday your time of troubles will end. Praise God for that day. In consoling you, God is preparing you to console others. Praise God by passing on the consolation that God has provided you.

Afterword

I am about to do a new thing; now it springs forth, do you not perceive it? I will make a way in the wilderness and rivers in the desert. (Isaiah 43:19)

People mark change in different ways. Before all this happened, when I dropped a bar of soap in the shower, I would think about how clumsy I was. During my time of troubles, when I dropped the soap, a series of practical questions popped into my mind related to what would happen to me if I ended up in prison. *Are the tiny bars of soap the Bureau of Prisons issues harder to hold onto than this one? Is there a way I can be less vulnerable to attack when I go to pick the soap back up? Would it be better if I just leave it there on the floor? Is there someone I can talk to in order to figure this out?* Nowadays, when I drop the soap in the shower, I think, *Wow! I used to spend a lot of time thinking about dropped soap.*

Mostly, this mental relaxation after the accusation is resolved is very welcome. However, after urgently seeking God and enjoying God's presence, I do not want to turn away when the source of urgency is removed. This turning away happens time and again in the Bible. The apostle Peter lamented it, citing the proverb, "The sow is washed only to wallow in the mud."

The change in your relationship with the LORD can be permanent. In fact, the turning toward God is supposed to be permanent. God is out to transform you and me. Jesus said we must be "born from above" or "born again." The apostle Paul underscored the depth of the transformation. "So," he wrote, "if anyone is in Christ, there is a new creation: everything old has passed away; see, everything has become new!"

Like any relationship, it requires work on both sides. On God's side, God seeks us out when we have turned away. God forgives us. As Paul said, God will actually change us to strengthen the relationship. The Psalmist prayed, "Create in me a clean heart, O God, and put a new and right spirit within me."

On our side, Jesus said, "If you love me, you will keep my commandments." Over the centuries since then, many have written wonderfully useful books about following Jesus and on the spiritual disciplines useful in cultivating closeness with God. To that library, I add one additional thought.

There is a sense in which an accused person is sharing the social experience that is at the very root of the Christian faith. From the beginning, the Christian tradition has been closely associated with the receiving end of the criminal justice system. John, who baptized Jesus, was executed in prison by the Jewish king Herod Antipas. Jesus was executed a few years later by the Roman governor Pontius Pilate. Peter and Paul, who proclaimed the teachings of Jesus throughout the Roman Empire, were both executed in Rome, probably by the Emperor Nero. The lists of Christian martyrs are still being compiled.

When you look, you can see the legacy of accusation, resistance, and comfort all through the teachings of the faith. The central Christian metaphor for the human condition is that we are each guilty of violating the law – despite our best efforts – and need redemption. At the end of time, "we will all stand before the judgment seat of God." The gospel of Jesus is not about the accusation; it is about help for the accused. As the hymn writer said, God comes to "rescue the perishing." At supper the night before he was executed, when Jesus described the Holy Spirit, which was to come after Jesus left the earth, he used the Greek word *parakletos*, which corresponds closely to the modern notion of criminal defense attorney. The "Advocate," Jesus promised his followers, will "be with you forever."

It is natural, then, that Jesus and his disciples directed compassion for prisoners. The writer of the letter to the Hebrews instructed, "Remember those who are in prison, as though you were in prison with them; those who are being tortured, as though you yourselves were being tortured."

Jesus put the matter even more starkly. He said that at the day of final judgment, those who visit "the least of these" who are in prison will "inherit the kingdom that is prepared...from the foundation of the world." On the other hand, those who do not visit "the least of these" who are in prison will "depart...into the eternal fire prepared for the devil and his angels."

My wife and I visited prison a few times through our church before I was accused. Since my acquittal we regularly participate in a Bible study at a men's prison. The men – who represent about 10 percent of the population of this unit – are wonderfully faithful and working hard to change their lives and ways of acting. They are humble and open.

The prisoners keep asking the volunteer team why we come to see them. We tell them the truth. We come to prison because we find God there.

Acknowledgments

I want to thank the friends and family who stood by me, helped my family in so many ways, and prayed for us. Your support meant more than I can express. Some have also helped me with these Meditations by carefully reading and thoughtfully commenting on various drafts. I want to give these readers special mention.

- Chaplain Al Gibbons had been through this wilderness and knew the way out. His openness with his faith and experience were a word from God to me. Al's wife, Sharron, is a constant and steadying presence.
- Sarah and John Seddelmeyer also provided extraordinary moral and physical support. I still cannot comprehend their generosity.
- Neal Stephens was one of my great trial lawyers. He was with me during each of the darkest moments of the legal proceedings.
- Reverends Barbara and Walt Marcum reached out and ministered to us with great sensitivity, despite the high protective walls I had thrown up.
- June and Steve Stock were the first readers of these Meditations, other than my wife. They are great encouragers. Their deep love for us is sustaining.
- William and Julie Ruehle gave us the first opportunity to talk about our experiences and, after Bill's acquittal, he blazed a path for the publication of these Meditations by writing and publishing a fascinating memoir of his own.
- My brother Steve Roberts added his enormous good humor and helped me honor my family heritage. Some of the most sacred parts of this experience I have shared only with him and my

wife. Steve's wife, Mari, was a charming advocate for constant revision.

- Dr. Mary Ann Little provided sanity checks, literally, and also counseled us to laugh.

- Linda Lucchesi, Professor Peter Lucchesi, Dave Kanne, and Pastor Phil Christensen read these Meditations without prior knowledge of the underlying events and provided great suggestions. Linda is a lifelong friend of my wife and another witness of her lionlike strength.

I have especially benefitted from the reading; care; honesty; support; and, above all, constant, selfless love of my wife, Dr. Susan Roberts. We lived this together.

All mistakes are mine, and I am solely responsible for the content of *The Strength of a Free Mind.*

$$* * *$$

After the case was over, a friend brought me a beautiful homemade cake. When I sliced into it, I found the two metal files she had baked into it. Ann, the files are sitting on my desk and still bring a chuckle.

References

Bible references are to the New Revised Standard Version (NRSV), unless otherwise indicated.

1 – 2   **"a reference to the ancient prayer"**: Psalm 19:14.

2   **"the view of a character in Charles Dickens's *Bleak House"*:** Charles Dickens, *Bleak House*, Oxford, U.K.: Oxford University Press, 1996, p. 777. *Bleak House* was first published in book form in 1853.

3   **"Lᴏʀᴅ, one who desires perfection must make it his first task"**: Thomas á Kempis, *The Imitation of Christ*, trans. Leo Sherley-Price, London: Penguin Group, 1952, p. 128. *The Imitation of Christ* was written c. 1418.

8   **"vague and amorphous on its face"**: *United States v. Brown*, 459 F.3d 509, 523 (5ᵗʰ Cir. 2006). I was indicted under the honest services statute, 18 U.S.C. §1346. A little over a year after my trial, the construction of the statute used in my indictment was struck down by the United States Supreme Court. *Skilling v. United States*, 561 U.S. 358, 130 S. Ct. 2896 (2010).

8   **"The Soviet novelist Vasily Grossman"**: Vasily Grossman, *Life and Fate*, trans. Robert Chandler, London: Vintage Books, 1980, p. 5.

8   **"The great Christian writer Thomas á Kempis"**: Thomas á Kempis, *The Imitation of Christ*, p. 45.

9   **"But with me it is a very small thing"**: 1 Corinthians 4:3 – 5.

11   **"a movie called *Freedom Writers"*:** *Freedom Writers*. Directed by Richard LaGravenese. Paramount Pictures, 2007.

12   **"he made anonymity 'the spiritual foundation'"**: *Alcoholics Anonymous*, 3rd ed., New York: Alcoholics Anonymous World Services, Inc., 1976, p. 564.

12 – 13   **"My basic flaw has always been"**: William Wilson, "The Next Frontier: Emotional Sobriety," The AA Grapevine, Inc., *Emotional Sobriety: The Next Frontier*, New York: AA Grapevine, Inc., 2006, p. 3.

13   **"Nevertheless many, even of the authorities"**: John 12:42 – 43.

16   **"The Psalmist prayed for me"**: Psalm 69:19.

16   **"It is good, too, that we sometimes suffer"**: Thomas á Kempis, *The Imitation of Christ*, p. 39.

17   **"I am the scorn"**: Psalm 31:11.

17   **"all deserted me"**: 2 Timothy 4:16.

17   **"You will all become deserters"**: Matthew 26:31.

18   **"Strike the shepherd"**: Zechariah 13:7.

18   **"Not just Peter"**: The story of Peter's actions during the trial of Jesus is found in Matthew chapter 26, Luke chapter 22 and John chapter 18.

18   **"Peter got up and ran"**: Luke 24:12 & John 20:6 – 7.

18   **"He 'put on some clothes"**: John 21:7.

19   **"[W]hen you grow old"**: John 21:18 – 19.

22   **"them which despitefully use you"**: Matthew 5:44 King James Version (KJV).

22   **"Sometimes I really do think"**: Barbara Kingsolver, *The Poisonwood Bible*, New York: Harper Collins, 1998, p. 516.

22   **"You shall not bear"**: Exodus 20:16.

22   **"You shall not spread"**: Exodus 23:1.

23   **"So you shall purge the evil"**: Deuteronomy 19:19 – 20.

23   **"[W]oe to that one"**: Mark 14:21.

25 – 26   **"Laurence Gonzales reports"**: Laurence Gonzales, *Deep Survival*, New York: W.W. Norton & Co, 2003, p. 164.

26   **"They were not to show the least consideration for us"**: Eusebius, *The History of the Church From Christ to Constantine*, trans. G. A. Williamson, London: Penguin Group, 1965, revised 1989, p. 267. *The*

History of the Church was written c. 323. The bishop quoted was Phileas, who was executed by the Romans in 307 A.D.

26   **"We must finish with them, not looking at their faces"**: Simon Sebag Montefiore, *Stalin: The Court of the Red Tsar*, New York: Alfred A. Knopf, 2003, p. 221.

26   **"No one...addressed a human word to you"**: Aleksandr Solzhenitsyn, *The Gulag Archipelago*, trans. Thomas P. Whitney, New York: Harper & Row, 1973, p. 181.

26   **"You have heard it said"**: Matthew 5:38 – 39, 41.

26   **"let your light shine"**: Matthew 5:16.

27   **"You are the light"**: Matthew 5:14 – 15.

29   **"they took Jeremiah"**: Jeremiah 38:6.

29   **"I have become a laughingstock"**: Jeremiah 20:7, 10.

29   **"My God, my God"**: Mark 15:34.

30   **"Do you still persist"**: Job 2:9.

31   **"The fugitive prophet Elijah"**: The quotes in this and the next two paragraphs are taken from 1 Kings chapters 18 – 19 NRSV & KJV.

33   **"Each person has a fight-or-flight response to danger."**: Daniel Goleman, *Emotional Intelligence*, New York: Bantam Books, 1995, p. 6.

33   **"Anger is more useful than despair"**: *Terminator 3: Rise of the Machines*. Directed by Jonathan Mostow. Warner Brothers Studios, 2003.

33   **"Do not be quick"**: Ecclesiastes 7:9.

33   **"You have heard that it was said"**: Matthew 5:21 – 22 New King James Version (NKJV).

33   **"[A]nger is the mood people are worst at controlling"**: Daniel Goleman, *Emotional Intelligence*, p. 59.

34   **"Be angry but do not sin"**: Ephesians 4:26.

34   **"slow to anger"**: Psalm 103:8.

34   **"Psalm 4:4"**: The first quotation of Psalm 4:4 is from the NKJV and the second is from the NRSV.

35   **"One who is slow to anger"**: Proverbs 16:32.

35   **"Whoever is slow to anger"**: Proverbs 14:29.

35   **"[D]o not let the sun"**: Ephesians 4:26 – 27.

35   **"President Eisenhower said, 'Don't go to war"**: Stephen Ambrose, *Eisenhower: The President*, New York: Simon & Schuster, Inc., 1984, p. 230.

37   **"Good men and bad men alike"**: Vasily Grossman, *Life and Fate*, p. 824.

38   **"For there is no distinction"**: Romans 3:22 – 23.

38   **"And the Pharisees and the scribes"**: Luke 15:2.

38   **"Those who are well"**: Mark 2:17.

38   **"Do you not realize"**: Romans 2:4.

39   **"Repent therefore"**: Acts 3:19.

39   **"Cast away from you"**: Ezekiel 18:31.

40   **"I had heard of you"**: Job 42:5 – 6.

42   **"It is my grief"**: Psalm 77:10.

42   **"Blessed are those who mourn"**: Matthew 5:4.

42   **"No one is finished – until he quits."**: Richard Reeves, *President Nixon: Alone in the White House*, New York: Simon & Schuster, Inc., 2001, p. 25.

42   **"The priest Henri Nouwen wrote,"**: Henri Nouwen, *Turn My Mourning Into Dancing*, ed. Timothy Jones, Nashville, Tenn.: Thomas Nelson, 2001, p. 56.

42   **"Jesus ran into a man"**: The quotes in this and the next paragraph are taken from John 5:2 – 8.

46   **"Frank Capra's classic movie *It's a Wonderful Life*"**: *It's a Wonderful Life*. Directed by Frank Capra. RKO Radio Pictures, 1946.

46   **"But he fully understood the monstrous pain"**: F. Dostoevsky, *Crime and Punishment*, trans. Richard Pevear & Larissa Volukhonsky, New York: Random House, 1992, p. 322.

48   **"Queen Jezebel issued a death warrant"**: 1 Kings 18:40 & 19:2.

48   **"sat down under a solitary broom tree"**: 1 Kings 19:4.

48   **"the great composer Ludwig van Beethoven told a friend,"**: Ludwig van Beethoven to Dr. Franz Gerhard Wegeler, 2 May 1810, *The Letters of Beethoven*, ed. & trans. Emily Anderson, New York: St. Martin's Press, Inc., 1961, Vol. 1, p. 270.

49	**"Jean Améry wrote,"**: Jean Améry, *At The Mind's Limits*, trans. Sydney & Stella Rosenfeld, Bloomington, Ind.: Indiana University Press, 1980, p. 25. Améry attributes the thought to Marcel Proust, who, he says, wrote it "somewhere."
49	**"this is the day"**: Psalm 118:24.
51	**"He got up, and ate"**: 1 Kings 19:8.
52	**"the pioneer and perfecter"**: The quotes in this and the next paragraph are taken from Hebrews 12:2 – 7.
52	**"On the forty-first day"**: 1 Kings 19:9 – 18.
53	**"Ironically, the man who once despaired"**: 2 Kings 2:11 – 12.
53	**"[R]un with perseverance"**: Hebrews 12:1.
56	**"I reread the story"**: The quotes in this and the next paragraph are from Genesis 39:20 – 23.
60	**"What others intend for evil"**: Genesis 50:20.
60	**"delivered me, because he delighted in me"**: Psalm 18:19.
60	**"The LORD sits enthroned"**: Psalm 29:10.
60	**"In the novel *Dead Souls*, Gogol asks,"**: Nikolai Gogol, *Dead Souls*, trans. Constance Garnett, New York: Barnes & Noble Books, 2005, p. 292. *Dead Souls* was originally published in Russian in 1842.
61	**"To experience humility"**: Laurence Gonzales, *Deep Survival*, p. 206.
61 – 63	**"He did what was right"**: The quotes in this and the next seven paragraphs are from 2 Kings 18:3 – 19:3.
63	**"deeply aware that God created him"**: Rudolf Otto, *The Idea of the Holy*, 2nd ed., trans. John Harvey, London: Oxford University Press, 1950, pp. 8 – 11. *The Idea of the Holy* was originally published in German in 1917 and first published in English in 1923.
63	**"The fear of the LORD"**: Proverbs 1:7.
64	**"The kingdom of God is"**: Mark 4:26 – 29.
64	**"That very night the angel"**: 2 Kings 19:35 – 36.
65	**"Thy will be done"**: Matthew 6:10 KJV.
65	**"How long will you go limping"**: 1 Kings 18:21.
66	**"idolatry is identified with greed"**: Ephesians 5:5; 1 Timothy 6:10.
66	**"No one can serve two masters"**: Matthew 6:24.

89	**"I am the true vine"**: John 15:1 – 5.
89	**"Do not say, 'Why"**: Ecclesiastes 7:10.
92	**"Sorrow is better than laughter"**: Ecclesiastes 7:3.
92	**"a time to weep"**: Ecclesiastes 3:4.
92	**"When God remade the promise"**: The quotes in this paragraph are from Genesis 17:17 and Genesis 18:12 – 15.
95	**"the singer Carrie Underwood had a huge hit"**: Hilary Lindsey, Gordie Sampson and Brett James, "Jesus, Take The Wheel" (2005).
96	**"How can one ever describe"**: Vasily Grossman, *Life and Fate,* p. 272.
96	**"San Francisco's Tenderloin District"**: The Tenderloin District of the City of San Francisco is the area south of Nob Hill and west of Union Square. It has been known for its high incidence of prostitution, drug addiction and violent crime. The origin of the name "Tenderloin" is not clear, but a similar area in New York City in the late nineteenth century bore the same nickname.
96	**"While on others you are calling"**: Fanny J. Crosby, "Pass Me Not, O Gentle Savior" (1868). Crosby's refrain reads, "Savior, Savior, hear my humble cry; while on others thou art calling, do not pass me by."
96	**"In the morning, while"**: Mark 1:35.
97	**"You have heard that it is said"**: Matthew 5:43 – 44.
97	**"Delivery me, O my God!"**: Psalm 3:7.
97 – 98	**"My times are in your hand"**: Psalm 31:15, 17.
98	**"No, 'if your enemies"**: Romans 12:20.
98	**"so that you may be children"**: Matthew 5:45.
98	**"Scripture reminds us that"**: Matthew 26:50 (Judas and Jesus) and Luke 23:12 (Herod and Pilate).
98	**"whoever wishes to be a friend"**: James 4:4.
98	**"[M]any live as enemies"**: Philippians 3:18 – 19.
98	**"For while we were weak"**: Romans 5:6, 10.
99	**"a Hindu proverb"**: A. L. Basham, *The Wonder That Was India*, 3rd ed., New Delhi: Rupa & Co., 1967, p. 451.
101	**"I had no plans, I said."**: Haruki Murakami, *The Wind-Up Bird Chronicle*, trans. Jay Rubin, New York: Random House, 1997, p. 194.

125	**"[H]ow often should I forgive?"**: Matthew 18:21 – 22.
126	**"a parable about a king"**: Matthew 18:23 – 35.
126	**"And forgive us our debts"**: Matthew 6:12 KJV.
126	**"James Woodward . . . . said,"**: Michael Hall, "The Exonerated," *Texas Monthly* November (2008): 165.
130	**"recall those earlier days"**: Hebrews 10:32 – 33.
130	**"Endure trials for the sake"**: Hebrews 12:7, 11.
130	**"[t]he Lord is my shepherd"**: Psalm 23: 1, 3.
130	**"Nothing is covered up"**: Luke 12:2.
131	**"[The Lord] heals the brokenhearted"**: Psalm 147:3.
131	**"Blessed are those who trust"**: Jeremiah 17:7 – 8.
133	**"beatings, imprisonments, [and] riots"**: 2 Corinthians 6:5.
133	**"imprisonments, with countless floggings"**: 2 Corinthians 11:23 – 25.
133	**"Blessed be the God and Father"**: 2 Corinthians 1:3 – 4.
134	**"the 'Wounded Healer'"**: Henri Nouwen, *The Wounded Healer*, Garden City, N. Y.: Doubleday & Co., Inc., 1972, p. 72.
137	**"The sow is washed"**: 2 Peter 2:22.
137	**"'born from above' or 'born again'"**: John 3:3 NRSV & KJV.
137	**"'So,' he wrote, 'if anyone"**: 2 Corinthians 5:17.
138	**"Create in me a clean heart"**: Psalm 51:10.
138	**"If you love me"**: John 14:15.
138	**"spiritual disciplines useful in cultivating closeness with God"**: The best introduction to the spiritual disciplines I have found is Richard J. Foster, *Celebration of Discipline*, San Francisco: HarperSanFrancisco, 1978, revised 1988.
138	**"we will all stand"**: Romans 14:10.
138	**"rescue the perishing"**: Fanny J. Crosby, "Rescue the Perishing" (1869).
138	**"the Greek word *parakletos*"**: John 14:16, 26; 15:26; and 16:7.
138	**"The 'Advocate,' Jesus promised"**: John 14:16.
138 – 39	**"Remember those who are in prison"**: Hebrews 13:3.
139	**"the least of these"**: Matthew 25:31 – 46.

Made in the USA
Lexington, KY
06 July 2016